The
HIDDEN PLACES
of
THE KENT

Edited by
Sean Connolly

Published by:
Travel Publishing Ltd
7a Apollo House, Calleva Park
Aldermaston, Berks, RG7 8TN

ISBN 1-902-00717-4
© Travel Publishing Ltd 1998

First Published: *1993*
Second Edition: *1996*
Third Edition: *1998*

Regional Titles in the Hidden Places Series:

Channel Islands	Cheshire
Cornwall	Devon
Dorset, Hants & Isle of Wight	Gloucestershire
Heart of England	Kent
Lake District & Cumbria	Lancashire
Norfolk	Northeast Yorkshire
Northumberland & Durham	Nottinghamshire
Peak District	Potteries
Somerset	South East
South Wales	Suffolk
Surrey	Sussex
Thames & Chilterns	Welsh Borders
Wiltshire	Yorkshire Dales

National Titles in the Hidden Places Series:

England	Ireland
Scotland	Wales

Printing by: Nuffield Press, Abingdon
Cartography by: Estates Publications, Tenterden, Kent
Line Drawings: Sarah Bird
Editor: Sean Connolly
Cover : Clare Hackney

Born in 1961, Clare was educated at West Surrey College of Art and Design as well as studying at Kingston University. She runs her own private water-colour school based in Surrey and has exhibited both in the UK and internationally. The cover is taken from an original water-colour of the picturesque village of Chilham.

All information is included by the publishers in good faith and is believed to be correct at the time of going to press. No responsibility can be accepted for errors.

Foreword

The Hidden Places series is a collection of easy to use travel guides taking you, in this instance, on a relaxed but informative tour through Kent - a mainly rural county often referred to as the *"Garden of England"* but possessing an extensive and varied coastline with very attractive upland and lowland countryside. This book contains a wealth of interesting information on the history, the countryside, the towns and villages and the more established places of interest in the county. But they also promote the more secluded and little known visitor attractions and places to stay, eat and drink many of which are easy to miss unless you know exactly where you are going.

We include hotels, inns, restaurants, public houses, teashops, various types of accommodation, historic houses, museums, gardens, garden centres, craft centres and many other attractions throughout Kent. Most places have an attractive line drawing and are cross-referenced to coloured maps found at the rear of the book. We do not award merit marks or rankings but concentrate on describing the more interesting, unusual or unique features of each place with the aim of making the reader's stay in the local area an enjoyable and stimulating experience.

Whether you are visiting the area for business or pleasure or in fact are living in the county we do hope that you enjoy reading and using this book. We are always interested in what readers think of places covered (or not covered) in our guides so please do not hesitate to use the reader reaction forms provided to give us your considered comments. We also welcome any general comments which will help us improve the guides themselves. Finally if you are planning to visit any other corner of the British Isles we would like to refer you to the list of other *Hidden Places* titles to be found at the rear of the book.

Contents

CHAPTER ONE
Mouth of the Medway

Cobham Hall

Chapter 1 - Area Covered

For precise location of places please refer to the colour maps found at the rear of the book.

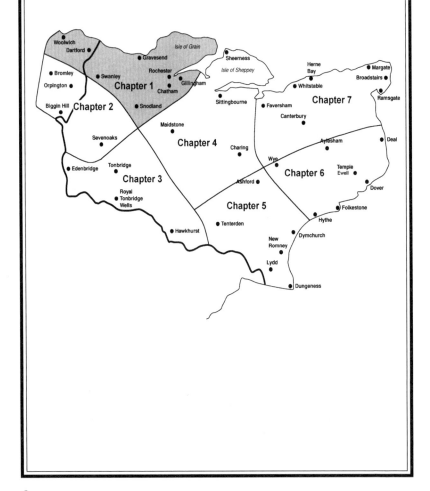

1
Mouth of the Medway

Introduction

The English can take a great sense of pride that Kent is the first county that most cross-Channel visitors encounter when visiting Great Britain. Few counties can combine its sense of regional identity, offbeat pronunciations, quintessentially English scenery and maritime history. Successive tides of invaders and visitors alike have left their legacies - from the ancient Romans to visiting EU officials - but beneath the veneer of modern development and change is a sense of timelessness and a stubborn Kentish outlook.

Nowhere has this traditional Kentish identity been more threatened than in its north-west corner, where London spreads inexorably eastwards along the Thames. Yet even in this semi-industrial corridor there is often a chance to find some architectural gem, a stretch of orchard or woodland, or a hidden hamlet where locals play old-fashioned Kentish games such as *bat-trap* at the village pub.

Three rivers define the landscape and history of this part of Kent. Foremost is the Thames, along which London-bound ships sail as far as Dartford where hey take on local pilots. Further east is the Hoo Peninsula, which juts far into the Thames Estuary with its coastal marshes giving way to cherry orchards and woodlands in the interior. At its base is a collection of communities - the Medway Towns - which take their name from the second of the great Kentish rivers. The dockyards at the mouth of the Medway were centres of ship-building since Tudor times, and places such as Rochester,

Chatham, Gillingham and Rainham all owe their growth to the marriage of Thames and Medway.

The Medway flows northwards through Kent, dividing the county roughly into east and west. To the west is the domain of Kentish Men; to the east traditionally live the Men of Kent. Distinctions like these mean a great deal and there is even a story of a motorist being stopped in a crowded London street for a succession of traffic offences. When told that the driver was up from Kent, the PC asked *"Kentish Man or Man of Kent"?* Hearing that the driver was a Man of Kent the policeman waved him on with just a friendly warning. Who knows what punishment might have befallen a Kentish Man?

The third main river of Kent - and also of this chapter - is the Darent. Like the Medway it flows northwards into the Thames. And like the Medway it provides an evolving landscape as it makes its way through narrow valleys northwards past the sites of Roman villas, Crusader hospitals, archbishops' palaces and Victorian railway viaducts.

Rochester

Late Victorian terraces and a steady flow of traffic are the first impressions many people have of Rochester. But as so often, first impressions can be incomplete or even misleading, and with some care and scrutiny the discerning visitor can peel layer after layer of history from this Medway port. With associations ranging from Celtic warriors to Charles Dickens, Rochester keeps cropping up in history books and in literary tomes.

The reason, of course, is location. Commanding a strategic situation by the mouth of the Medway - and therefore with easy links to the Continent via the Thames - Rochester was first settled more than two millennia ago. The first known inhabitants were Celts of the Belgic tribe. Then it was the turn of the Romans, whose Watling street crossed the Medway at this point. The Romans fortified their camp here, thereby creating a walled city of nearly 23 acres. Some five centuries later the settlement came under Saxon dominion, and at this time it acquired the name which would - with some alteration - become permanent: *Hrofesceaster*. Rochester later became linked with two famous kings. Alfred, determined to thwart Viking sea power, built a fleet of ships in Rochester and in doing so created England's first navy. The strategic importance of Rochester was not lost on a famous subsequent ruler, William the Conqueror who decreed that a castle be maintained there permanently. ***Rochester Castle***, built by William's chief architect, Bishop Gundulph, stands as a testament to centuries of defence. Henry I ordered the massive keep to be raised and this huge edifice still stands as a symbol of Rochester. Towering 120 feet high and with walls up to 12 feet thick, it comprises four floors with many openings looking out. It was here, in 1215, that rebel barons were besieged by King John for seven weeks. The barons withstood a fusillade of stones thrown by huge siege engines but it was only after a tunnel was built beneath the keep, and its props burnt to cause a collapse, that the castle surrendered. Rochester Castle was severely damaged during the Civil War and much of today's structure is the result of extensive restoration in the last century.

Near the castle stands ***Rochester Cathedral***, which was also built by Bishop Gundulph. It occupies the site of a Saxon church, which is significant because the Bishopric of Rochester is the second oldest in England, having been established in the 7th century. Like the castle it was badly damaged by Parliamentary troops dur-

Rochester Cathedral

ing the Civil War and underwent a restorative treatment in the 19th century. Nevertheless there is still a great deal of original Norman, gothic and 15th century work still in evidence. Particularly noteworthy are the Norman west doorway, the 13th century transepts and the 13th century crypt which has heavy ribbed vaulting.

The remains of former monastic buildings surround the Cathedral, and there are three ancient gates: **Priors Gate**, **Deanery Gate** and **Chertsey's Gate**, which leads on to the High Street. It is more popularly known as Jaspers Gate, the name under which it appeared in Dickens's last (unfinished) novel, *The Mystery of Edward Drood*.

Rochester makes the most of its Dickens connection, and it provides the setting for scenes in *Great Expectations, Pickwick Papers* and *The Uncommercial Traveller*. Each year there is a Dickens Festival, during which an assortment of Dickens characters wander the streets in Victorian costume. Eastgate House is the home of a popular and informative **Dickens Centre**, and in its garden is the chalet in which the great writer wrote in his last years. Many of the sights mentioned in his novels are linked along the **Charles Dickens Trail**. Following this walking tour is also a good way to appreciate some of the 17th and 18th century architecture along Rochester's High Street, and to spend some time in the docks which also feature in some works by Dickens.

Where River meets the Sea

Cobham   *Map 2 ref E3*
4 miles W of Rochester off the A2
Cobham is a picturesque village which is famous for its half-timbered **Leather Bottle Inn**, which figures in *The Pickwick Papers*. It was here that Tracey Tupman was discovered by Mr Pickwick after having been jilted by Rachel Wardle. The village has a history that goes much further back than the Dickensian era, though, and there have been traces of the Roman occupation found around here.

The parish church of **St Mary Magdalene** was built in the 13th century and enlarged in the 14th. On its floor are more than 18 brasses, which are reckoned to be the best in England. They commemorate members of the Cobham family and were produced over two centuries in the late Middle Ages. Behind the church are **almshouses** which incorporate a 14th century kitchen and hall. They were once part of the Old College, built by the 3rd Lord Cobham;

he endowed them as living quarters for five priests who were to pray for the repose of his soul. In 1537, after the Dissolution of the Monasteries, the College was suppressed and it assumed its present use for almshouses in the 17th century.

Cobham Hall, one of the great houses of Kent, was built in the last two decades of the Elizabethan period. Its wings retain the features of late Tudor architecture but its great hall was rebuilt in the 17th century and substantially enlarged in the late 18th and early 19th centuries. It contains some excellent work by Inigo Jones and the Adam brothers. It is now a girls school and is sometimes open to the public.

Cobham Hall

The lovely red-brick house known as **Owletts** was bought by a Cobham farmer in the late 17th century and it retains a charming sense of rural comfort. Although it has an imposing staircase its real appeal is in its modest proportions and its beautiful garden.

The **Darnley Arms,** which is the oldest pub in Cobham, is an 18th century building although there has been an inn on this site for 600 years. During those years it has experienced many upheavals, and it is reputedly haunted by one Sir Thomas Kemp, who was

The Darnley Arms

executed in the 15th century and spent his last night at this inn. Today the pub is the haunt of walkers, cyclists, and Rotary club members, all of whom are welcomed by the popular landlords, Trevor and Beryl Howard. There is a traditional beamed ceiling and a beamed former hay loft which is now used for functions. The best things about this pub, though, are what is missing - music, juke box, cigarette machines - so that patrons can enjoy a drink or one of the fortifying meals without tiresome distractions. Fresh fish is a particular speciality. The Darnley Arms enjoys an unusual distinction in being licensed to conduct marriages on the premises. *The Darnley Arms, 40 The Street, Cobham, Kent DA12 3BZ   Tel: 01474 814218*

Strood

Map 2 ref F3

1 mile W of Rochester on the A2

Strood is one of the Medway towns on the opposite side of the river facing Rochester. It is known mainly for the **Temple Manor**, built by the Knights Templar in the early 13th century. Later it became a nunnery until it was suppressed by Henry VIII in the 16th century. For several centuries it served as a farmhouse, growing gradually more dilapidated until its restoration after the Second World War. It contains a 13th century hall on a vaulted undercroft. This, as well as the 17th century brick extensions are some of the oldest original elements of the building, which has been sympathetically restored.

Upnor   *Map 2 ref F2*
3 miles N of Rochester on the A228

With a river frontage along the Medway and backed by wooded hills, Upnor has become something of a resort for the people of the Medway Towns. Apart from its role as a leisure centre Upnor has an impressive **castle**, which is really like a fortified manor house, with turrets and crenellation. It was built in 1561 to protect the Medway and the approaches to Chatham. Despite its commanding location and appearance it never proved very effective. The castle performed dismally in 1667 when it offered a lacklustre defence against the Dutch fleet under de Ruyter. The Dutch made their way up the Medway, destroying several men-of-war before sailing away. One of the guns which performed so ineffectively against the Dutch was salvaged from the river and now stands guard outside the entrance to the fort.

Cooling   *Map 2 ref F2*
11 miles N of Rochester off the A228

Cooling is an isolated village in the heart of the Hoo Peninsula, which juts out into the Thames Estuary north of Rochester. There are woodlands and orchards around Cooling, but the landscape becomes more barren by the shore, edged with marshes and wind-bent trees. **Cooling Castle**, although not open to the public, can be seen very clearly from the road. Twin drum towers guard the gate and there is a moat visible by the massive walls. Cooling Castle was built in the 14th century and was later the home of Sir John Oldcastle, who was hanged in 1417 as a Lollard - one of the supporters of John Wyclif whose preachings were fore-runners of Protestantism. Notwithstanding Sir John's support for clerical poverty, he was said to be the model for Shakespeare's Falstaff.

North of Cooling, but accessible only by footpath, lie the **Halstow Marshes**, which attract bird-watchers especially in the winter. The marshes and water meadows are nesting sites and feeding grounds for many water birds, including several species of duck and white-fronted geese. **Northward Hill Bird Reserve** is Britain's largest heronry, although access is very restricted and by permit only.

Allhallows

Map 2 ref G2

9 miles N of Rochester off the A228

Allhallows has a remote quality, exposed as it is at the end of the Hoo Peninsula and looking across the Thames at the much busier Essex resort of Southend. There is a beach resort by the sea wall and a curious stone obelisk at the mouth of Yantlet Creek marks the limit of the authority of the Port of London over the River Thames. Nearby is an *iron beacon* erected in Elizabethan times, one of many such beacons set along the coast to warn of imminent invasion. The railway station, built in Art Deco style in 1932, was closed when Allhallows failed to attract the expected influx of tourists. It now serves as a shop.

Grain

Map 2 ref II2

15 miles N of Rochester off the A228

Grain marks the end of the line on the Hoo Peninsula, or more precisely the Isle of Grain at its eastern end. Its main attraction is its sweeping view of the Thames Estuary, but many visitors are put off by the profusion of refining tanks industrial smells emanating from the oil refinery and power station that stand nearby.

Chatham

Map 2 ref F3

1 mile E of Rochester on the A2

Although a settlement existed here in Anglo-Saxon times, Chatham was a sleepy backwater until Henry VIII established a dockyard. The dockyard flourished and expanded under Elizabeth I and it continued to grow for the next four centuries. During that time many famous ships were built in Chatham, including Nelson's Victory, which was launched in 1765. A scale model of the famous ship can be seen in the Council Chamber of the *Town Hall*. The naval connection lay behind the steady growth of Chatham and its present commercial centre originally saw to the needs of naval personnel. Among these was on John Dickens, who was employed by the Nay Pay Office. His son Charles spent some of his boyhood years in Chatham. The house where he lived, *No 2 Ordnance Terrace* (now no 11), stands among a group of handsome 18th century houses.

Chatham Historic Dockyard, located just north of the town centre, tells the story of Chatham's naval history. Visitors can trace the rise of the Royal Navy from the days of the squat Tudor ships to the sleek lines of today's nuclear submarines. Set strategically on a hill overlooking the docks is Fort Amherst, which was built in 1756 as part of the defensive structure of the Royal Naval Dockyards. There is an impressive gatehouse as well as storerooms, powder rooms and a labyrinth of tunnels burrowing inside the hill itself. Historical re-enactments take place on most Sunday evenings in the summer. To the south the urban feel of Chatham soon gives way to rolling, wooded countryside.

Few pubs are named so unusually - and yet at the same time as logically - as **The Waggon at Hale**. The hamlet of Hale was once the end of the coaching road to Chatham, the alternative being the steeply graded Chatham Hill. Horse-drawn vehicles would stop at Hale and then a message would be sent to nearby Brickfields, announcing that *"the waggon is at Hale"*. The name has stuck, as has the pleasantly rural feel to Hale despite its being within easy strik-

The Waggon at Hale

ing distance of Chatham and Gillingham. The pub itself seems to contribute to the pleasant atmosphere of the valley; outside there is ample parking and a large garden with children's play area, a pergola and a barbecue area. The interior is taken up by the huge open-plan bar and eating area. The beams above contain delightful quotes from Dr Johnson and other wits, while log fires blaze in the winter. There is a great atmosphere, with quizzes, Halloween nights, and summer fetes among the attractions; meals are served lunchtimes. *The Waggon at Hale, 179 Capstone Road, Luton, Chatham, Kent ME5 7PP Tel: 01634 400624*

Gillingham
Map 2 ref F3

2 miles E of Rochester on the A2

The largest of the Medway Towns, Gillingham developed alongside its neighbour Chatham as a centre for servicing the naval dockyards and depot. Gillingham has much earlier traces, including evidence of prehistoric and Roman settlement. It became a manor under the Normans but only began to grow once the ship-building industry developed nearby.

The parish **Church of St Mary** stands on The Green in the heart of the oldest part of town. Traces of its Norman origins are visible inside where the two pillars in the chancel are from the early 12th century. The font is - also dating from that period - an interesting feature, since it was built large enough for total immersion.

Gillingham is lucky to possess one of the most fascinating military attractions in the country, in the form of the **Royal Engineers Museum of Military Engineering**. The museum is a cornucopia of memorabilia, containing exciting displays of real equipment and many working models. The ingenuity displayed in many military engineering projects had beneficial knock-on effects for civilian life; early diving equipment and a 1915 smoke helmet are good examples. In addition to the practical equipment there is a wealth of unusual military mementoes such as the Dragon Robe awarded to *"Gordon of Khartoum"* after his successful campaigns during the Tai Ping rebellion of 1864. The medal gallery evokes the heroism and ingenuity of the Royal Engineers, succinctly expressed in their two mottoes - *"Ubique"* (Everywhere) and *"Quo Fas et Gloria Ducunt"*

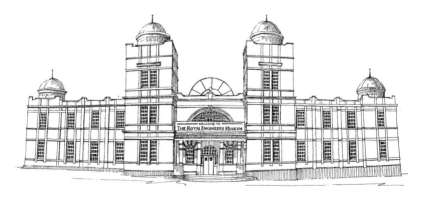

Royal Engineers Museum of Military Engineering

(Where Glory and Honour Lead). *The Royal Engineers Museum of Military Engineering, Prince Arthur Road, Gillingham, Kent ME4 4UG   Tel: 01643 406397*

Rainham
Map 2 ref G3
4 miles E of Rochester off the A2

The parish church of **St Margaret in Rainham**, once a separate village but now incorporated into Gillingham, dates mainly from the 14th and 15th centuries, but there is also some interesting Norman work visible. Inside are the traces of some interesting Medieval murals as well as the remains of six consecration crosses.

Offering a chance for a pleasant stop on the outskirts of Chatham and Gillingham is **The Rose Inn** in the village of Rainham, a popular and welcoming pub. Mrs Lesley Mitchinson manages the Rose with flair and creativity, providing the many local regulars with a social nerve centre while always making sure that visitors can settle in easily. To say the pub is popular locally is something of an

The Rose Inn

understatement, considering that it plays host not only to its own football team but to six darts teams. Weekly quiz nights in the winter add a note of good-natured competition. A large U-shaped bar serves the entire pub, which has a lovely open fire and an atmospheric assortment of brasses and pictures on the walls. Two of its recent Shepherd Neame awards - as winner of the Cellar Competition and of the Pub Food Award - indicate Lesley's skills both behind the bar and in the kitchen. *The Rose Inn, 249 High Street, Rainham, Gillingham, Kent ME8 8DR Tel: 01634 231047*

A Taste of the Downs

Luddesdown   *Map 2 ref E3*
5 miles SW of Rochester off the A227

Luddesdown is set in the northern flank of the North Downs, where wooded hills begin to give way to the farming country of lower levels. Really no more than a hamlet, Luddesdown has a remote feel, and it can only be reached by narrow lanes or footpaths. One such footpath leads southwards through wooded hills to the tiny village of **Dode**, which was deserted at the time of the Black Death. Another leads through a narrow valley known as the Bowling Alley to **Holly Hill**, one of the highest points in Kent and commanding fine views. Luddesdown parish church has some interesting Roman tiles in its tower walls. Just by the church is **Luddesdown Court**, reputed to be one of England's oldest inhabited houses.

Meopham   *Map 2 ref E3*
8 miles SW of Rochester on the A227

Newcomers to Kent - and especially foreigners - should take a crash course in the pronunciation of Kentish place-names. The correct pronunciation of some seems to bear no resemblance to their spelling; others manage to turn an unlikely jumble of letters into something perfectly easy to manage. Meopham (pronounced "*Meppam*") fits into both categories. It is a pretty village, strung along the A227, which is known as the Wrotham Road in these parts. A well-maintained cricket green is visible from the road and there is a preserved **windmill**. Meopham was the birthplace of the great 17th century naturalist and gardener John Tradescant, who introduced many non-native species of flowers and vegetables to England. Meopham also acts as a trading centre for a number of outlying villages as it is the largest settlement between Longfield and Borough Green.

Just to the south of Meopham in the lovely hamlet of **Harvel** is the setting for the **Amazon and Tiger**, a freehouse that attracts walkers, cyclists, and music lovers as well as a good cross-section of Harvel society. An outdoor patio overlooks the village cricket ground and there is a special children's play area. The mellow interior is festooned with hop bines and the tables and seats - all purchased from sales and auctions - are conversation piece in themselves. Pride of place goes to the wide choice of real ales coming from all over the United Kingdom, but licensees Mike and Lesley Whitehouse also oversee some fine home cooking. They also organise live music and

The Amazon and Tiger

there are special jazz evenings on the first Wednesday of each month. Mick is the person to ask about the origins of the pub's name. *The Amazon and Tiger, David Street, Harvel, Near Meopham, Kent DA13 0DE Tel: 01474 814705*

Stansted   Map 1 ref D4
14 miles SW of Rochester off the A20
Both the M20 and A20 pass within about a mile of Stansted, and yet the village manages to convey a sense of remoteness and tranquillity. It has a lovely setting in the undulating hills of the North Downs, with broad views either looking north towards Gravesend and the Thames Estuary or southwards towards Wrotham Hill and the Weald in the distance. A campsite located about a mile south of the town is popular with spectators at Brands Hatch, which is about 3 miles north of Stansted, but a million miles away in terms of noise and commotion.

With an elevated location in the village of Stansted that lives up to its name, ***The Hilltop***, a club, restaurant and hotel has built up a loyal and appreciative following. Mrs Joan Sefer has run the Hilltop as a family business for more than 35 years but the building has capitalised on its position since the 1800's, when it was known as Brattles. Its address - Labour in Vain Road - probably earned its name in that era, as the hill was notoriously difficult for horses to climb.

These days guests can comfortably pull in to the large car park and pop into the Theatre Bar with its animated atmosphere and assortment of celebrity photographs. Daren Sefer, Joan's son, stud-

The Hilltop

ied at Westminster College and this training underpins his skill as chef/manager of the restaurant. The Hilltop provides a variety of special interest nights - light opera is a favourite midweek. A night-club runs at weekends. Accommodation is comfortable and welcoming, either in the hotel rooms with their four-posters or in the holiday chalets for those with a yen to stay longer. *The Hilltop Club Restaurant Hotel, Labour in Vain Road, Stansted, Sevenoaks, Kent TN15 7NY, Tel: 01732 822696/822481 Fax: 01732 824089*

Wrotham
Map 1 ref D4

13 miles SW of Rochester off the A20

Seemingly oblivious to the M20 which passes just to the north is Wrotham (pronounced *Rootum*), an ancient village which once served as a staging post on the London road. It was here that Henry VIII received news of the execution of Anne Boleyn in 1536. Wrotham parish church of St George would have been more than three centuries old at the time. It is large and airy, perhaps because the village once had a palace belonging to the Archbishops of Canterbury. The heart of Wrotham, next to the church, is its compact village square which has two very old pubs, a brick manor house and the remains of the archbishop's palace.

One thing is unique about **The Three Post Boys**, which is set right in the square opposite Wrotham's parish church - no other pub in the UK bears the same name. Indeed the pub seems to relish its unusual nomenclature because its menus, cards, and other printed material all feature the same motif of three scarlet-jacketed horn blowers. The name derives from Wrotham's position on the old London to Dover mail route. It was from here, where the Three Post Boys lived in the attic room, that the mail was delivered to the surrounding areas.

The Three Post Boys

This is a traditional inn dating back to the 16th century. Drinking mugs hang from the beams of the open-plan bar and carriage lamps recall the days of the old mail route. Greene King real ales are a speciality along with good-quality bar meals. In the summer months the extensive beer garden and covered patio are a welcome retreat for ramblers, cyclists, and families alike. The tenants Ron and Jacqui Clift offer a warm welcome to all. *The Three Post Boys, The Square, Wrotham, Kent TN15 7AA Tel: 01732 780167*

Trottiscliffe
Map 2 ref E4
12 miles SW of Rochester off the A20
Trottiscliffe, as its written name implies (it is actually pronounced "*Trosley*"), occupies a hillside situation. It lies just to the south of **Trosley Country Park**, which can be reached by taking one of the

many well-marked walks from the village. Trottiscliffe itself is a tidy, pretty little village with views over the Downs that lured the artist Graham Sutherland into living in the village. His house, in true Kentish weatherboard, is near the centre of the village. ***Trottiscliffe parish church*** occupies a magnificent setting, flush against the steep downland hillside.

A series of paths and tracks leads from the church up to the plateau behind Trottiscliffe. Here, commanding a fine eastward view over the Medway Valley, are the ***Coldrum Stones***, a magnificent archaeological site. Some 24 columns, each of a huge stone, once marked the perimeter of a circular long barrow some 50 feet in diameter. Only four of the original stones are still standing, and a huge burial mound inside the circle has disappeared, but what remains is evocative and mysterious. The columns measure up to 12 feet by 10 feet and are not of local stone. The Coldrum Stones have been maintained by the National Trust since 1926, some 16 years after it was excavated.

Vigo Village
12 miles SW of Rochester off the A227
Map 2 ref E4

Vigo Village lies along the ridge known as the ***North Downs Way*** that runs east from Wrotham. It is a recent addition to the area, having been built on the site of a Second World War camp in the midst of a chestnut woodland. As such, it is more noteworthy for its location and views than for any intrinsic architectural merits. Just to the south lies ***Trosley Country Park***, where a network of paths and nature trails snake their way through 160 acres of woodlands and more open chalk downland. The visitor centre provides details of three circular waymarked trails, one of which leads to the Coldrum Stones near Trottiscliffe.

Burham
5 miles S of Rochester off the A229
Map 2 ref F4

Burham is set on slopes in the upper Medway Valley; above it the

Kits Coty House

Downs reach one of their highest points at ***Bluebell Hill***. However, Burham is noted for a man-made structure - a remarkable archaeological site known as ***Kits Coty House***. Like Coldrum Long Barrow about 4 miles west across the Medway Valley, Kits Coty House represents the remains of a

Neolithic burial chamber. It is smaller than Coldrum Long Barrow but is better preserved, its capstone still in place across the three huge upright stones. As is so often the case with Neolithic monuments it commands far-reaching views, looking out across the valley towards the Medway Gap.

West towards the Capital

Gravesend
Map 2 ref E2

7 miles W of Rochester on the A226

Gravesend marks the point at which ships entering the Thames - some half a mile wide at this stage - take on a river pilot for the journey upstream. It is a busy maritime community, with cutters and tugs helping maintain a steady flow of river traffic. It is the river, with its bustle and atmosphere, that provides the attraction in Gravesend, partly because most of the old buildings were destroyed in a fire of 1727. Among the buildings lost to fire was the parish **Church of St George**, which was rebuilt in a handsome Georgian fashion. The churchyard marks the final resting place of Pocahontas, the daughter of a Native American chieftain who reputedly saved the life of English settler John Smith in Virginia. Pocahontas was brought to England but died aboard ship on a journey back to Virginia. A life-sized statue marks her burial place in the churchyard.

Statue of Pocahontas

Dartford
Map 1 ref C2

12 miles W of Rochester on the A296

Dartford is a built-up, urban settlement known to most people chiefly for the **Dartford Tunnel**, which travels roughly one mile beneath the Thames, re-emerging on the Essex bank near West Thurrock. However, Dartford has a great deal of historical significance. It stands on the old London to Dover Road at the crossing of the River Darent

- its name actually means *"Darent Ford"*. It was also in Dartford that Wat Tyler assembled his band of rebels in 1381. The local council has helped keep a sense of proportion in Dartford by making its high street a car-free zone. This measure has made it easier to appreciate some of the remaining old buildings such as the **Bull Inn**, with its galleried courtyard, a relic of coaching days. The parish **Church of the Holy Trinity** dates from the late 11th century. During restoration work in the 19th century an interesting 11th century wall painting was uncovered.

Swanscombe
Map 1 ref D2
10 miles W of Rochester on the A226

Swanscombe was the site of an important archaeological find earlier this century when fragments of a human skull were found in a gravel pit in 1935. Analysis of the bones indicated an age of about 200,000 years, making them some of the oldest human remains found in Europe. This riverside settlement also has remnants of more recent historical periods; its parish church dates mainly from the 12th century but incorporates bricks from the Roman times and parts of its tower predate the Norman Conquest. Although the church was substantially restored in the 19th century, making it difficult to detect which are the original features, it does provide a tangible evidence of the many layers of human settlement here along the Thames.

Stone
Map 1 ref D2
1 mile E of Dartford on the A226

The village of Stone, which is very much on the outskirts of Dartford, has a particular gem in its **Church of St Mary**, which according to local tradition , was built by the masons who worked on Westminster Abbey. The reason for this assertion seems to lie in the similarity of appearance between the interiors of the two churches. St Mary represents a marvellous example of Gothic architecture, with its lofty nave, double arcade of piers and vaulted roof. In addition there is excellent carving throughout the church.

Sutton at Hone
Map 1 ref D3
4 miles S of Dartford on the A225

Sutton at Hone is one of the last villages in the Darent Valley before the river flows into the Thames at Dartford. Here, some 5 miles from its mouth, the river still manages to retain a pleasing appearance despite hints of the built-up landscape that lies ahead. Manfully fighting a rearguard action against any traces of urban life is **St**

Johns Jerusalem, a lovely manor house set right at the edge of the village. It was built in the 12th century as a commandery of the Knights Hospitallers; parts of this original building are visible in the present manor house. The river flows around the house itself, giving it a moated appearance. St Johns Jerusalem is maintained by the National Trust, and the garden and chapel are open to the public.

The Greyhound is a pub with a central location in the rural village of Sutton at Hone, near Dartford. Some 250 years old, it presents a solid appearance along the road, its traditional white-faced exterior adorned with colourful hanging baskets. This is an example of that lucky sort of pub that presents a welcoming face to strangers while maintaining a strong local clientele. The interior is small and inti-

The Greyhound

mate, with brasses and prints lining the walls and comfortable seating throughout. There is usually a game of darts or cribbage under way, and the several pool tables widen the choice of games inside. To the rear is a pretty beer garden with ample seating surrounding the ornamental cherry tree in the centre. The home-cooked food includes tempting daily specials. The Greyhound is handy for the local fishing lakes and riverside walks. *The Greyhound, Sutton at Hone, Dartford, Kent DA4 9EU   Tel: 01322 862228*

Darenth and South Darenth

Map 1 ref D3

4 miles S of Dartford off the A225

The villages of Darenth and South Darenth lie south of Dartford and unlike their neighbour Sutton at Hone they have something of an urban, or at least developed, feel. That, however, does not stand against them since they contain a number of curious buildings and edifices which conjure up images of vigorous Victorian building programmes. In Darenth itself is a massive **hospital**, which must rank as one of the largest ever built. Fronting the road for a full half mile it was built as an asylum, which says something about the *"care in the community"* ideas of the last century.

South Darenth has a railway pedigree, and its **railway viaduct**, presenting a ghostly silhouette against the setting sun, is famous. The tallest structure is a mill chimney, another reflection of Victorian industry. Many houses in South Darenth were bought up by British Rail in the 1980's because it was thought that they would be threatened by the Channel Link railway.

The two buildings that make up **The Jolly Millers** pub in South Darenth present an interesting appearance to a passer-by. The lower building, with the main entrance, is a handsome white-faced and brick combination, while the adjoining section has a flint frontage. This type of blending of building materials often suggests great age and the Jolly Millers fits the bill exactly - its bar area dates from the 14th century. The pub was formerly a charnel house and stood on glebe land; the dining area (behind the flint frontage) was originally

The Jolly Millers

the stables. The interior backs up this sense of age with its original beams and interesting vaulted ceiling in the dining area.

The pub is popular with the local fire brigade, which explains the abundance of fire-fighting memorabilia among the old photographs and fittings. The Jolly Millers keeps a good range of real ales and serves bar meals at lunchtime; evening meals must be booked ahead. Outside is a large garden with a bat and trap pitch and a good-sized children's area. *The Jolly Millers, 1 East Hill, South Darenth, Kent DA4 9AN Tel: 01322 862167*

Bexleyheath
Map 1 ref C2
3 miles W of Dartford on the A207

Located as it is between Dartford and Woolwich, Bexleyheath would seem to be very much an urban affair, yet it does contain a number of surprises. Its name is a clue to its history, and it was a genuine heath until it was enclosed in 1814. Subsequent development throughout the 19th and early 20th centuries tamed the wild nature of the landscape, although it preserves a good amount of parkland as a bulwark against the tide of terraced houses.

Bexleyheath's local retailing importance was confirmed with the recent construction of a covered *shopping centre*. Although strictly utilitarian in the purpose it is meant to serve, the centre has a tall car park, and from the top there are outstanding views looking north towards the Thames docklands and south towards the greener expanses of the rest of Kent. *Danson Park*, in the heart of Bexleyheath, is one of these areas and represents an oasis of greenery.

Standing proudly in what amounts to a park-within-a-park is *The Danson Stables*, which must be the most impressive pub in Bexleyheath. A central section, devoted mainly to seating for diners, is flanked by two wings. The beauty of a pub as expansive as the Danson Stables is that one wing is totally no-smoking while the other has no such ban. The stables themselves were built around 1800 to serve Danson Mansions - the size of these former stables is a reflection of the estate's importance. English Heritage had a hand in the painstaking restoration of the stables to their present magnificent condition. The central area has flagstone floors while the two wings have bare wood. Despite the scale and spaciousness of the interior, there is a cosy feeling about the pub: authentic old paintings hang above old wooden furniture and logs are stacked by the original fireplaces. With a good range of beers and wines and a comprehensive menu of food served all day, the Danson Stables is a

The Danson Stables

gem of a pub. *The Danson Stables, Danson Park, Bexleyheath, Kent DA6 8HL   Tel: 0181 303 3168*

It's worth making a special diversion to Bexley itself to sample some of the excellent food on offer at ***Filled of Dreams***. The sporting pun in the shop's name is not far off the mark as the sandwiches, filled baguettes, rolls and other luscious savouries on offer here tempted members of the London Broncos American football team to

Filled of Dreams

make Filled of Dreams a favourite refuelling stop. Owner Mark Grout is personable and welcoming, somehow making the small premises seem as broad as his smile. Customers can eat at one of the small tables inside and there is more seating to the front in good weather. A wide range of breads, including ciabatta and hearty wholemeal loaves, are displayed on shelves by the counter. Customers can select both the bread and the fillings - of which there are more than 20 varieties - to create their own choice. Filled of Dreams has a devoted local following and a reputation for high quality and friendly service. *Filled of Dreams, 7 Village Way, Beckenham, Kent BR3 3NA Tel: 0181 658 8455*

Chislehurst   *Map 1 ref B2*
5 miles SW of Dartford on the A208

Chislehurst developed as one of London's more select suburbs, tempting new residents with its mix of fresh air and a hint of the downland scenery further into Kent. It has managed to remain relatively unspoilt by further development, thanks in large part to the **common**, which remains an oasis of greenery despite being criss-crossed by a number of roads. Just to the south of the centre is a golf course - the house on it was the last home of the ex-Empress Eugenie of France.

The golf course is on the way to the attraction that draws most visitors to Chislehurst. **The Chislehurst Caves** are one of Britain's most interesting archaeological wonders, and visitors can join guided tours to explore them. The first stop is the Map Room, where it becomes clear that the system, which is entirely man-made, com-

The Chislehurst Caves

prises three sections, each of which coincides with a historical era. The oldest, known as the Druids, dates back approximately 4,000 years. The largest section of the system, excavated some two millennia later, is the Romans. The smallest - and youngest - of the sections is the Saxons, excavated some 1,400 years ago. The caves are full of fascinating traces of these layers of history, as well as evidence of more recent events.

Cavaliers took refuge in the caves during the Civil War, and there is a pit that was built to impale their Roundhead pursuers. At the height of the Blitz, during the Second World War. Chislehurst Caves became Britain's largest air raid shelter, with up to 15,000 people protected there at a time. Informative guides are happy to answer questions about these and other aspects of the caves, which tunnel some 22 miles overall through the countryside. *Chislehurst Caves, Old Hill, Chislehurst, Kent BR7 5NB   Tel: 0181 467 3264*

CHAPTER TWO
The Surrey Borders

Chartwell

Chapter 2 - Area Covered

For precise location of places please refer to the colour maps found at the rear of the book.

2
The Surrey borders

Introduction

This, the chapter covering the smallest area of Kent, might seem to be at a disadvantage. Moreover, it is one of only two not to include any of Kent's extensive coastline. Added to these considerations, it is bisected by the M26 and M25. Yet despite these seeming handicaps, the relatively compact area around Sevenoaks is full of interest, with natural wonders, archaeological monuments and architectural gems seeming to crop up around every bend.

Near Ide Hill, the wonderful undulating paths of Emmetts Garden blanket the forested ridge that forms the highest point in Kent. From here the views take in vistas that stretch in all directions. It is from this upland region that the Darent begins its journey northwards, flowing and sometimes swelling as it passes lovely North Downs villages such as Otford, Shoreham and Eynsford. This is a countryside worthy of a lyrical poet, with castles and Roman ruins dotted amongst the wooded hillsides.

Blending in with the rural charms of this area are a number of historic houses, some great and others more modest. Chartwell, Sir Winston Churchill's country home near the Surrey border, commands views over the Weald of Kent. Just to the north, in Westerham, is Quebec House, rich with memories of General James Wolfe. Ightham Mote is surrounded by its own peaceful mote, tucked in a narrow valley in the woodlands south of Sevenoaks. And in Sevenoaks itself is a mansion of surpassing stature and grace - Knole House, which for many people is reason enough to visit Kent, let alone this one modest area of it.

Sevenoaks

With its easy rail and road access to London and its leafy atmosphere Sevenoaks has come to epitomise the essence of the commuter belt in many people's eyes. This perception is not far from the truth but far enough away to reveal a genuine community with its own sense of history and identity. The leafiness is not that of a garden city creation, designed to soften the effect of wide-scale residential and commercial development. Instead it is a testament to the wooded countryside which formed the backdrop of this settlement some nine centuries ago.

It is believed that there was a settlement on this site in ancient times but the first recorded mention came in AD 1114 when a record of local churches listed it as *"Seovenaca"*. Local tradition has it that the name refers to a clump of seven oaks that once stood here, long gone but replaced - with much fanfare - by seven trees taken from Knole Park and ceremoniously planted on the common on the outskirts of town in 1955. These replacements gained national headline status in 1987, when they suffered badly during the Great Wind of October.

The rural feel of Sevenoaks - struggling against the odds - parallels the story of those trees. Despite the commuter tag which it must bear, Sevenoaks still has the appearance of a country market town, and it holds weekly cattle and produce markets not far from the station. A number of traditional Kentish tile-hung cottages, as well as a fine Regency pub and some grand houses, still line the main street before it assumes a more anonymous aspect.

Located at the north end of Sevenoaks on the A225 next to Sevenoaks Hospital is **Puddleduck Quilters**, where visitors can pass through ordinary shop front doors to enter the delightful and colourful world of quilts and wallhangings. Chris and Lesley organ-

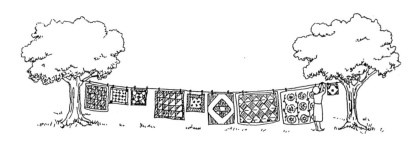

Puddleduck Quilters

ise a range of patchwork and quilting courses on the premises, aimed at people of every level of experience and ambition. Courses run from one day to ten weeks in duration, at the end of which time most people are *"hooked"* on this fulfilling and therapeutic pastime. The shop sells an array of fabrics, and everything for the patchworker and quilter, all representing excellent value. *Puddleduck Quilters, 116 St John's Hill, Sevenoaks, Kent TN13 3PD Tel: 01732 743642*

Not far from the centre of Sevenoaks, however, are further reminders of the town's heritage. **The Vine cricket ground** lies on a rise to the south of the town centre. It was given to the town in 1773 but the first recorded match at the Vine - between Kent and Sussex - took place in 1734. It witnessed a remarkable match in 1782 when the Duke of Dorset (one of the Sackvilles of Knole) and his estate-workers defeated a team representing All-England. The victory was particularly sweet because the Duke's team also won a bet of a thousand guineas.

Set just south of the main street and, opposite Sevenoaks School and the famous Knole House, is **The Royal Oak Tap**, one of the most animated pubs in the area. The attractions of this free house are its intriguing mix of customers featuring students, sportsmen and foreign visitors to the sights nearby. The pub, which was built in the 16th century, was once a blacksmiths and is now a listed building. Inside, the *"Tap"* is open plan, with stone floors, a large inglenook fireplace and old carvings on the bar frontage. As well as substantial lunches there is a good selection of cask ales and wines; manager Julian Mitchell organises barbecues to coincide with sat-

The Royal Oak Tap

ellite TV events. The Royal Oak Tap scores highly, for a town pub, in having its own car park. *The Royal Oak Tap, 3 Upper High Street, Sevenoaks, Kent TN13 1HY Tel: 01732 458783*

The pride of Sevenoaks, and of Kent itself for many people, is of course **Knole House**, the huge manor house set in extensive parkland. It is one of the largest houses in England, with 365 rooms inside its foursquare structure.

Knowle House

The present house stands on the site of a much smaller manor house which was bought by the Archbishop of Canterbury in 1456 and used as an ecclesiastical palace until 1532 when it was taken over by Henry VIII. Elizabeth I granted it to the Sackvilles, who still live there although the house is now owned by the National Trust. Impressive in its scale, Knole House also offers visitors the chance to wander past outstanding collections of tapestries, antique furniture and an extensive art collection which has masterpieces by Gainsborough and Reynolds.

The great house is not without its sense of human involvement. The Sackvilles proved to have the flair for employing the best craftsmen to realise their creative architectural spirit. The writer Vita Sackville-West was born in Knole House in 1892; some five decades later Hitler intended to use it as his English headquarters.

Surrounding Knole House is its majestic deer park, covering some 1000 acres of rolling countryside with dense beech woodlands giving way to hidden dells.

From Sevenoaks to Orpington

Kemsing *Map 1 ref D4*
3 miles N of Sevenoaks off the A225

Lodged below the southern slopes of the North Downs, Kemsing manages to retain much of its original charm despite its nearness to the M26 and the village's expansion to reflect its attraction as a commuting base. The village centre has a number of old-style tile-hung cottages and a *youth hostel* now occupies the former vicarage. From here it is possible to make a number of pleasant walks into the surrounding hills.

One walk, a 3 mile circuit, leaves *Green Hill*, near the centre of Kemsing. It passes *Hildenborough Hall* before rising on to Whiteleaf Down. Walkers are rewarded by the sight of The Rising Sun, an old-fashioned pub which is nestled among a scattering of farm buildings. From here and elsewhere along the walk, there are sweeping views across the Kent countryside. A well-marked footpath leads directly back to the village.

Otford *Map 1 ref C4*
3 miles N of Sevenoaks off the A225

Otford makes the most of its pleasant location along the banks of the *River Darent*. Water plays a part in the atmosphere of the village, which has a lovely duck pond in its centre. Like so much of this area of Kent, Otford has a history that stretches back to Roman times and beyond. There are Roman remains all along the surrounding Darent Valley.

It became an important cross-roads in the centuries that followed as well. It was here in AD 774 that King Offa of Mercia fought against the men of Kent. Henry VIII stopped in Otford on his way to the historic encounter with Francois I of France at the Field of the Cloth of Gold, staying the night in one of the many palaces belonging to the Archbishop of Canterbury. The palace, now reduced to a few sections of wall, stood beside the church of St Bartholomew, which stands facing the duck pond at the heart of the village. *The pond* is something of a historical curiosity, having been documented as early as the 11th century. It is said to be the only stretch of water in England to be classified as a listed building.

Located snugly in the heart of Otford High Street is *The Studio*, a gallery that is full to the brim with paintings, ceramics and other objets d'art. For owner/manager Wendy Peck, running the Studio is both a labour of love and a chance to put her training in fine arts to good use. Wendy is keen to offer information about the pieces for sale, which include a wide range of watercolours, oils, pastels and collage in addition to sculptures, jewellery, textiles and handsome ceramics. She is a fine painter herself and specialises in watercolours and oils of landscapes. Commissions of portraits can also be arranged. In fact, the idea of the Studio came from Wendy's ambition to have a showcase for her own work as well as

The Studio

a space to paint. The studio space is in the bright upstairs workshop, where Wendy can also see to other sides of the business such as a useful framing service. *The Studio, 20 the High Street, Otford, Kent TN14 5PQ, Tel: 01959 524784*

Shoreham   Map 1 ref C4
4 miles N of Sevenoaks on the A225

The River Darent runs alongside the village of Shoreham, and on the hillside across the valley there is a large cross carved into the chalk, commemorating those who died in the two world wars. The river features prominently in the village, with footpaths running along it and a handsome **hump-backed bridge** crossing it. Near the bridge is **The Water House**, in which Samuel Palmer lived for seven years. Palmer was a great friend of the poet and visionary William Blake, who visited him here.

The **Shoreham Aircraft Museum** houses an exhibition of aviation memorabilia from the Battle of Britain as well as the other aerial engagements over southern England during the Second World War. The funds raised by the museum are used by the Shoreham Aircraft Preservation Society for aircraft recovery work and to support the RAF Guinea Pig club for airmen suffering severe burns.

Standing on more than three acres of lovely gardens and shielded from the village lane by a hefty yew hedge, **Church House** is a

Church House

restful and tranquil B&B. The house itself is Georgian, dating from around 1750, although the Victorian frontage - first seen when entering through the graceful yew archway - is Victorian. The four guest rooms, one of which is en suite, are spacious and handsomely decorated. There are lovely views out over the grounds and the surrounding countryside. Downstairs is a private drawing room for guests, decorated with several Georgian touches.

Kate Howie, the owner of Church House, can trace the Howie name back to the 12th century. She is good company and enjoys talking about history with guests. Much of this history has a decided gardening slant to it - not surprising since Kate has a degree in the History, Design and Maintenance of Gardens in addition to her qualifications in hotel and catering management. The extensive gardens, which are at the guests' disposal, feature ponds, an interesting gazebo, and an all-weather tennis court. A short walk takes visitors to the five local pubs and the local rail station with its connections to London. *Church House, Church Street, Shoreham, Sevenoaks, Kent, Tel/Fax: 01959 522241*

Set among the fine old houses of Shoreham village is **Ye Olde George Inn**, a 600 year-old pub that attracts a good mix of local villagers and visitors. The address - Church Street - is stretching things a bit, because it is not much more than a lane, although parking is not a problem. The overhanging, timbered upper floor is a giveaway to the pub's age, as are the low ceilings in the open plan interior. Open fires blaze in the winter and customers can take a

Ye Olde George Inn

seat at the pew-style benches and old tables or settle into a high-backed stool at the bar, with its unusual twisted wrought iron rail. Ye Olde George is a free house, with a good selection of real ales and wines by the glass. Its restaurant section specialises in fish, including unusual choices such as swordfish, barracuda and mahi-mahi. There is also a good selection of lighter bar food available. The pub makes a good base for exploring the village and adjoining countryside, and the former cottage of water-colourist John Palmer is only 100 yard away by the river. *Ye Olde George Inn, Church Street, Shoreham, Sevenoaks, Kent TN14 7RY Tel: 01959 522017*

Eynsford   Map 1 ref D3
8 miles N of Sevenoaks off the A225

The centre of Eynsford manages to preserve a sense of history, with a number of timber-framed houses and the church's tall shingled steeple rising above the busy A225. It is only by going down a side-street, however, that the visitor can appreciate the real charm of this village nestled cosily along the banks of the Darent. It is here that visitors come across the ford which gives its name to the village. The *ford* is passable by cars although a depth chart to the side indicates that water levels can rise as high as six feet when the river is swollen with floodwater. The Darent is also crossed by a hump-backed bridge, similar to that in Shoreham, and a brick-built viaduct that carries the Swanley to Sevenoaks railway line.

Eynsford Ford

At the end of the lane is a modern building which nevertheless houses one of Kent's most important archaeological treasures: ***Lullingstone Roman Villa***. The villa was only uncovered in 1949 although its existence was known since the 18th century when farm labourers uncovered fragments of mosaics which had been pierced when the labourers had driven fence posts into the ground. Not as large as some other Roman remains, Lullingstone is noteworthy in being extremely well preserved, allowing the visitor not only to trace the history of the building over four centuries but also the style of life adopted by wealthy country families in Roman Britain.

A glass and timber pavilion protects the excavated villa from the elements and visitors can examine all the elements that made it a whole, including the main living rooms, the deep room, the original bath -house - with colourful mosaic flooring throughout. The deep room contains relics of pagan worship but the villa also has a Christian chapel - the only example of a chapel found within a private Roman villa in Britain.

Farningham
Map 1 ref D3

10 miles N of Sevenoaks on the A225

Farningham, another Darent Valley village, was once on the main London road, and much of the Georgian architecture in the village centre reflects the trading prosperity that such a location bestowed. Today, however, it is lucky not to be on the main London thoroughfares - the M20 and the A20 - both of which pass near by but far enough away to allow Farningham to retain a sense of its own identity. The 13th century church, along the high street, has been extensively restored but does have an interesting eight-sided font inscribed with the sacraments - the number of sacraments being seven since the carving was done in pre-Reformation times. A handsome 18th century brick bridge stands by lawns that slope down to the river's edge. Alongside the river runs the **Darent Valley Path**, which follows the course of the river as far as Dartford. It must be said, however, that Farningham offers some of the last genuinely unspoilt riverside scenery. Exploiting the riverside location is a lovely weatherboarded **mill**, which, with its cottage, fronts a lawn that also runs down to the river itself.

Biggin Hill   *Map 1 ref B4*
12 miles W of Sevenoaks on the A233

Biggin Hill, is best known for its association with the RAF and in particular its role in the Battle of Britain. A Spitfire and Hurricane flank the entrance to **Biggin Hill RAF Station**, silent reminders of the stalwart service these aircraft put in during the dark days of the Second World War. A chapel in the Air Station commemorates the 453 pilots stationed in Biggin Hill who gave their lives during the War. The location of Biggin Hill itself, high on a plateau on the North Downs, made it an obvious choice for an airfield. The views over the Darent Valley, particularly along the Westerham Road leading south, are outstanding. The village itself, which sprawls along this plateau, is more noteworthy for its setting and military history than for any intrinsic architectural beauty although there is one notable curiosity - **St Mark's Church**, which was built almost single-handedly by the local vicar between 1955 and 1959 using material from the derelict All Saints Church in Peckham.

Located just outside the centre of Biggin Hill village is **Jeannette's Hobby Ceramics**, one of a group of small shops with a neighbourly feel. Jeannette Leese, the owner, loves ceramics and set up her first shop in 1992. *"Hobby ceramics"* is an American idea which has crossed the Atlantic successfully, providing a fulfilling and enjoyable way for people to make their own decorations and mementoes. Jeannette is an enthusiastic supporter of this pastime and she can explain just how newcomers to the art can use moulds and paints to produce ceramic works of the highest quality. She offers courses which run for several hours on weekdays and Saturdays, with up to 16 students learning how to make the most of her 1,400 moulds in order to further their own creative ends. Jeannette provides all the equipment and after teaching the basics is on hand to

Jeannette's Hobby Ceramics

advise students; she also offers a firing service for the completed moulds. *Jeannette's Hobby Ceramics, 12 Rosehill Road, Biggin Hill, Westerham, Kent TN16 3NF   Tel: 01959 570540*

Downe

Map 1 ref B4

11 miles NW of Sevenoaks off the A233

The village of Downe, which lies high up on the Downs near Biggin Hill, has a commanding setting with fine views, especially looking north towards London. Its appearance reflects its position at the cross-roads - in more ways than one. The central core of traditional Kentish flint cottages fights for survival against the rising tide of anonymous suburban housing spreading southwards from the capital.

Even its natural setting, still evident in the outskirts of the village, is poised between the open uplands of the downs themselves and the more wooded areas of Kent such as the Weald further south. But more than any landscape Downe is associated with one man, and by extension to *"Man"* himself. It was here, in **Down House** that Charles Darwin lived for 40 years until his death in 1882. During that time the great naturalist analysed his findings from his voyages on the *Beagle*, wrestled with his Anglican conscience, and eventually produced the work that changed the way we looked at ourselves and our evolution - *On the Origin of Species*. The house, now owned by the Royal College of Surgeons and run as a Darwin museum, reflects much of its former owner's character. It has been painstakingly restored as it was in Darwin's time. Rambling though it might be, this is no comfortable country bolt-hole. In fact it would seem that the great scientist denied himself many of life's pleasures while attending to the matters of Life itself.

Just outside the beautiful village of Downe is **Christmas Tree Farm**, where visitors can come in close contact with Betty the Cow and her assortment of farmyard friends, including sheep, goats, chickens, geese, ponies, donkeys, and pigs. Children love these animals and there is an enclosed pet area with smaller animals such as goslings, chicks, rabbits, chinchillas, and guinea pigs. Some of these

Christmas Tree Farm

animals are for sale and many families go home with a new member. In addition there is a wide range of shrubs and plants for sale, plus hanging baskets and rustic garden furniture. The landscaped gardens contain a fish pond as well as the Tea Gardens, where cream teas and other refreshments are available. Parking is convenient in the large car park. *Christmas Tree Farm, Cudham Road, Downe, Near Orpington, Kent BR6 7LF   Tel: 01689 861603*

Bromley   Map 1 ref B3
18 miles N of Sevenoaks on the A264

Despite its present role as a market town swallowed by Greater London, Bromley has a distinctive character. Its name means *"glade in the broom"*, an evocative title perhaps for a centre that saw a great deal of rebuilding after extensive bomb damage in the Second World War. Much of the town is given over to modern high street-style shopping, and there is also an enclosed shopping centre. Bromley, however, is not without some surviving older elements. Bromley College is the name given a group of 17th century almshouses, which stand not far from the parish church, with its medieval tower. Countryside with a more rural aspect begins just south of Bromley as the land begins to undulate on its way to the North Downs.

Set in a distinctive Tudor-style building in the village of Locksbottom, on the outskirts of Bromley, is **Chapter One**, a top-quality restaurant which, having opened in 1996, has already won high praise and commitment from its customers. It is hard to put a finger on just what it is that Chapter One does to get things right each time. Perhaps it is the attentive service, or the sense of flair

Chapter One

and imagination that is the secret ingredient of each item on the menu. Inside, the restaurant uses warm, sunny colours, soft fabrics and wooden stained glass partitions to create modern, spacious and comfortable surroundings. There is a separate bar area for a pre-dinner drink or a casual lunch from their interesting brasserie menu. The restaurant menu uses classic French and English dishes and gives them a modern twist - without introducing unnecessary fussiness. The result matches the surroundings - tasteful and refreshing, and a clever marriage of the traditional and the up-to-date. *Chapter One, New Fantail Building, Locksbottom, Farnborough, Kent BR6 8NF Tel: 01689 854848*

West of Sevenoaks

Sundridge
Map 1 ref C4

3 miles W of Sevenoaks on the A25

Sundridge provides a wonderful counterpoint to some of the Darent Valley villages downriver from it such as Shoreham, Eynsford and Farningham. Here the river, which further north threatens to overflow its banks during prolonged rains, is nothing more than a narrow stream. The village is pretty enough, just south enough to have avoided too much encroachment from London, but the best thing about Sundridge is its setting amid hills to the north and south. One of the best views southward over the Weald of Kent is from the look-out at **Ide's Hill**, reached by a small lane from the centre of Sundridge. The hills to the north of the village reveal equally majestic, if rather different, views. Below, stretching northwards towards London and the Thames Estuary, are green fields and meadows. Almost overlooked in the verdure are the major trunk roads and motorways that traverse northern Kent, all but swallowed up as if the Green Movement had waved a magic wand over the expanse.

Brasted
Map 1 ref C5

5 miles W of Sevenoaks on the A25

The lovely village of Brasted lies along the Darent, which at this stage is still quite narrow. Almost reflecting the miniature nature of the river, the village presents a snug, cosy appearance. At its heart is a well-kept, compact village green, which is flanked by a row of attractive cottages which date back to the Tudor period. An exception to this small-scale tableau is **Brasted Place**, which was designed by the great Robert Adam - and is one of only two houses in Kent to have been designed by him. The mansion gained fame in the early 19th century when Prince Louis of France (later to become Napoleon III) spent some time there before leading a group of supporters back to France in 1842. Brasted Place is now used as a training college.

An inn has stood on the site of **The White Hart** since 1386, although today's welcoming establishment was built as a coaching

The White Hart

inn in 1825 and enlarged in 1885. A large car park stands beside the pub, which presents a handsome exterior to motorists as they enter the lovely village of Brasted. The White Hart has been modernised tastefully but many of the original Victorian features remain, including beautiful old-fashioned fireplaces with mirrors. Polished wooden floors, scrubbed oak tables and a profusion of plants and flowers give it a country feel, while manager Gwyn Kennett and his staff help create a warm and friendly atmosphere.

The White Hart prides itself in its Great British food - served all day every day. Customers can choose from a range of hearty dishes with the emphasis on freshness and good value. The White Hart was a popular haven for RAF pilots from Biggin Hill during the Battle of Britain, and there are photographs and books recalling those heroic days. These days customers are more likely to take off for some of the attractions nearby such as Knole, Chartwell and Hever Castle. *The White Hart, High Street, Brasted, Kent TN16 1JE, Tel: 01959 560651*

Ide Hill
Map 1 ref C5

6 miles SW of Sevenoaks off the B2042

Ide Hill is a small village in the upper Darent Valley which draws visitors in with a series of subtly changing views. Most people climb - by foot or by car - into the village. Before them, and still somewhat higher up, is the village green and the church. Venturing past the church the visitor is presented with a view which changes in scale considerably. Looking south, past the verdant trees and shrubs in the foreground, one can enjoy a sweeping panorama of the Weald stretching off into the distance. A network of bike and walking trails encircles the village, providing a similar combination of pleasant close-ups and dramatic vistas glimpsed between the trees and high hedges. Just outside Ide Hill, and set in a hillside of mature beech trees, is **Emmetts Garden**, whose National Trust-maintained gardens are open to the public on certain days throughout the summer. A 100 foot Wellingtonia, planted on the highest point in Kent (some 700 feet above sea level), stands over this 5 acre garden which is renowned for the variety of its trees.

French Street
Map 1 ref C5

7 miles SW of Sevenoaks off the B2042

A tiny hamlet, tucked in the folds of narrow wooded hills, French Street has the appearance of one of the most out of the way spots in Kent. In fact, many people arrive here by foot - and possibly by chance - as it suddenly appears round the bend of one of the footpaths that traverse the neighbouring woods.

Rustic and unprepossessing French Street may be, but it is also on the doorstep of one of the county's most beloved attractions, **Chartwell**, the country home which Winston Churchill bought in 1924. When Churchill bought it, Chartwell was a modest house commanding a splendid view across the Weald. He set about enlarging

Chartwell

the house, helping it to match the magnificence of its view. But the work was not designed to magnify Churchill's own sense of importance. Instead the newly built wall and landscaped gardens enabled him to find precious hours of diversion, occupying himself with the horticulture of the estate or in painting by its lake. The National Trust maintains Chartwell and have successfully captured the spirit of the great statesman in the painstakingly preserved rooms. There is a real sense of his presence here, especially in the studio and in his library.

French Street is also a good starting point for visiting a more poignant sight, ***Toys Hill***, which can be reached by following a footpath from the village through dense beechwoods. Toys Hill is also a National Trust property, comprising 200 acres of woodland which once surrounded a house known as Weardale Manor. The woodlands themselves were devastated by the hurricane-force winds of 16 October 1987, when south-eastern England felt the full force of the winds coming up from the Channel. Huge and ancient beech trees were felled or even snapped and the scene the next morning was one of almost total devastation. There has been an intensive replanting scheme in operation since the Great Storm, and new beeches are taking root on the brow of the hill. In the meantime there are marvellous views past where the great trees once stood.

Crockham Hill   *Map 1 ref B5*
9 miles SW of Sevenoaks on the A269

Crockham Hill stands on the slopes of the Greensand Ridge. Greensand is a porous rock which easily soaks up rain water. Combined with a subsoil layer of clay, the rock combination makes for unstable conditions on ground level. The surface of the surrounding meadows is peppered with strange hummocks and dips, which rise and fall according to the weather and the water levels below. Some four centuries ago there was a dramatic landslip, which altered the surrounding topography permanently. Overnight, hedges and hills were swallowed, replaced by new hillocks and depressions.

The village itself seems remarkably unmoved by the permutations of the landscape, and there are three famous gardens located in Crockham Hill. ***Larksfield Cottage***, which was redesigned in 1981, features expansive lawns, shrubs and views over the Weald and the Ashdown Forest. ***Larksfield*** was the home of Octavia Hill, one of the founders of the National Trust. She helped to create a garden which has a collection of azaleas, shrubs, herbaceous plants, roses and woodlands - all with dramatic views over the Weald. ***The Red House*** is a handsome property where the owners have withstood the temptation to create a formal garden and instead have concentrated on rolling lawns flanked by trees and shrubs including rhododendrons, azaleas and magnolias. One of the most pleasant features of the Red House is the rose walk which leads visitors to the gardens themselves.

Westerham   *Map 1 ref C5*
9 miles W of Sevenoaks on the A25

Westerham is one of the westernmost communities in Kent, tucked against the Surrey border. The building of the M25, just a mile or so north of Westerham, eased the town's traffic congestion considerably and it now has a calmer aspect more in keeping with its former days as a coaching station. The town lies between two upland areas, with the North Downs to the north and Greensand Ridge - the source of the River Darent - just to the south.

In the main street and around the tiny green of this small town are a number of old buildings, including two venerable coaching inns. The centre of the town, by the green, has statues of two British heroes with Westerham connections. General James Wolfe, victor of the decisive battle between the English and French at Quebec in 1759, was born in Westerham. The house where he grew up, built in the 17th century but renamed **Quebec House** in honour of his famous victory, stands to the east of town and is maintained by the National Trust. There are household items and other memorabilia relating to Wolfe on display, and in the stable block there is an exhibition about the Battle of Quebec.

Another mansion of the late 17th century, **Squerryes Court** also has Wolfe connections. Wolfe was a friend of the Warde family who owned this William and Mary house. It was here that Wolfe received his first commission in 1741 - at the age of 14. The house has a collection of paintings by the Dutch Old Masters, period furniture and tapestries, as well as a special room set aside for Wolfe exhibits. The Darent rises in Squerryes Park, which extends back from the house past formal gardens.

A pair of attractive old lamps flank the front of **The Old House at Home**, along the narrow road that enters Quebec Square along Vicarage Hill. *"Old house"* this pub certainly is, having served thirsty wayfarers and villagers for hundreds of years. Appealing decor adds character to this popular pub, which stocks a range of real ales as well as Kent favourite Shepherd Neame. Leaded stained glass windows, framed by brocade curtains, cast a timeless light on the distinctive oak panelling on most walls. Brasses, a post horn and dozens of hanging mugs strengthen the feeling of being in a country

The Old House at Home

hostelry. Log fires generate warmth and a mellow glow in the winter and solid, comfortable chairs line the bar. Jacqui and Michael Morris manage the Old House at Home with an unassuming confidence, and they are good sources of local knowledge despite being somewhat recent arrivals in Westerham. Mealtime specials, which change regularly, are listed on the blackboard and there is ample parking to the side of the pub. *The Old House at Home, Quebec Square, vicarage Hill, Westerham, Kent TN16 1TD*

It is hard to resist pausing for much-needed refreshment at **The Coffee Garden**, a cosy spot that makes an ideal stop for a light lunch or a reviving coffee or tea. Proprietor Nicky Dempsey offers a

The Coffee Garden

homely welcome to her no smoking establishment, which has the feel of a country kitchen - with tantalising aromas to match. There is a wide range of teas, including tisanes and herbal infusions, but the coffees are the star turns here. Most of the twelve varieties are served either by the cup or by the larger bowl - a real treat. The menu gives good descriptions of the choices, which include a number of delicious flavoured coffees such as Rich Hazelnut, Irish Cream and Caribbean Rum. The food menu ranges from hearty all-day breakfasts to soups, sandwiches and hot dishes such as shepherds pie, pasta bakes and filled jacket potatoes. The Coffee Garden is also licensed to serve wine, cider and beer. And the garden that lends its name to the operation? That is a snug hideaway behind the shop, with wrought iron tables and chairs stretched along a sunny patio. *The Coffee Garden, 19 High Street, Westerham, Kent TN16 1RA, Tel: 01959 561706*

Oxted   Map 1 ref B5
12 miles W of Sevenoaks on the A25

It is worth crossing westwards into Surrey to visit Oxted, an old town that prospered because of its position just below the Downs and consequently a good trading link with the rest of Surrey. Today, however, Oxted constitutes two distinct parts. New Oxted lies between the original town and Limpsfield to the east; it grew up around the railway station which was built in the 19th century. Old Oxted is also largely Victorian to the eye, but occasionally the visitor notices some survivors of earlier centuries such as the **Forge House** and **Beam Cottages**, with their medieval core and 17th century exteriors. **Streeters Cottage**, built in the 17th century, presents a large timber-framed gable to the road.

Staffhurst Wood   Map 1 ref B5
10 miles W of Sevenoaks off the B2026

The Royal Oak is located in the attractive village of Staffhurst Wood near Oxted. On the outside it is the quintessential English pub, with leafy vines trailing down the shingled upper storey and a timber-frame gable. Tables, a children's play area and a spacious patio are geared to summer barbecues and there are views over three counties - Sussex being the third. Inside is a lovely marriage of English and French cultures, with real ale, darts and open fires setting the scene for a Gallic-inspired menu. Sondrine Costanzo and Sebastien Gayet learned their trade in their native France and have been manager and chef of the Royal Oak since 1994. Specialities such as moules marinieres, paupiette of guinea fowl and pan-fried pork fillet Normandie have a distinctly cross-Channel flavour. The best of British is also represented with roast duck, smoked chicken salad and pan-fried red mullet. An imaginative selection of wines, including some inspired New World choices, rounds off an excellent meal. *The Royal Oak, Staffhurst Wood, Oxted, Surrey RH8 0RR Tel: 01833 722207*

The Royal Oak

Limpsfield and Limpsfield Chart   Map 1 ref B5
10 miles W of Sevenoaks off the A25

The churchyard at Limpsfield, just into Surrey, contains the grave of the composer, Frederick Delius, who despite having died in France, left instructions that he should be buried in an English country grave-yard. **Detillens**, a rare 15th century *"hall"* house, is also located in Limpsfield. This striking building has an unusual *"king-post"* roof, and despite having been given a new facade in the 18th century, is a good example of a house belonging to a Surrey yeoman, a member of the class of small freeholders who cultivated their own land; in-side, there is an interesting collection of period furniture, china and militaria.

Limpsfield Chart, or simply **The Chart**, constitutes a hilltop common with some lovely views eastwards across Kent. Next to the common is a 17th century **Mill House**; the windmill itself was re-moved in 1925. Elsewhere in The Chart there are handsome groupings of stone-built houses, cottages, and farm buildings, best exemplified by the ensemble at Moorhouse Farm.

The Chart is the home of **Joyces-on-the-Chart**, a memorable tea room that also serves light lunches and occasional evening meals. It has a lovely location in the Chart, a charming little village near

Oxted, full of stone-built cottages and sunny gardens. Such a setting is defiantly uncommercial, and Joyces-on-the Chart - which also has an amazing selection of greetings cards - is the last remaining shop still open in this village. It's not hard to understand its staying power. The setting is romantic, with its handsome awning announcing its presence. Inside is some of the best-cooked food available for miles around,

Joyces on the Chart

ranging from home-made soups and broths to steak, seafood and vegetarian specialities. For many of its repeat customers, though the high point is the traditional cream tea or simply a good filter coffee accompanied by a rock bun, Danish pastry or home-made cake. The garden is a tranquil oasis from the world's cares. *Joyces-on-the-Chart, Post Office Row, The Chart, Oxted, Surrey RH8 OTH Tel. 01883 722195*

East of Sevenoaks

Shipbourne   *Map 1 ref D5*
5 miles SE of Sevenoaks on the A227

Shipbourne is another Kentish village that traps unwary visitors, at least with its pronunciation: locals say "Shibbun". It is a quiet, unassuming village that blends in well with the lovely surrounding countryside - which seems to suggest the Weald further south. Several walking trails lead from the centre of Shipbourne into the environs; one particularly pretty trail leads from the church and its adjacent oast-houses through a narrow valley and eventually to Ightham Mote.

Plaxtol

Map 1 ref D5

5 miles E of Sevenoaks off the A227

A row of traditional Kentish weatherboard cottages flanks the side of the parish church of Plaxtol, a hilly village occupying a prominent location on the ridge near Ightham Mote. Just to the east of the village, and reached through a circuitous succession of narrow lanes, is **Old Soar Manor**, a manor house built in the 13th century. The house occupies the solar block of the original building, which served as a knight's dwelling. Of particular interest are the undercrofts below it, with graceful vaults curving upwards.

The setting of Old Soar Manor is idyllic, with orchards and copses surrounding it. The woods grow more dense as they climb the ridge rising up from the orchards; at the top is one of southern England's largest forests, **Mereworth Woods**. Wild boar once roamed through its oaks and beeches, although today the wildlife is of a tamer variety.

Even closer to Plaxtol, but in the opposite direction from Old Soar Mansion, is **Ightham Mote**, one of England's finest Medieval manor houses. This gem of a building, owned by the National Trust, is set in a narrow wooded valley roughly halfway between Plaxtol and the even smaller village of **Ivy Hatch**. A moat surrounds the house, although the name *"mote"* probably refers instead to an Old English word meaning *"meeting place"*.

Ightam Mote

Ightham Mote was built in the 14th century, with its central court-yard retaining the meeting-place purpose. The outside walls, above the moat, are of soft ragstone, which catches the evening light with a warm glow. The construction inside utilised great amounts of local oak, with massive timbers still very much in evidence in the rafters and central hall (the solar), as well as in the main staircase, built in Jacobean times.

Kent's lucky position on the doorstep of France is exploited at **The Plough**, an attractive pub in the tiny hamlet of Ivy Hatch. Chef-manager Daniel Humbert imaginatively blends his own Gallic savoir-faire with some of the freshest ingredients to be found in Britain. The setting for this entente cordiale is a stone-and-shingle pub very much in keeping with the Kent landscape. Picnic tables dot the patios and gardens front and back and the welcoming inte-

The Plough

rior features large open fires, old oak tables and church pew seating in the bar area. Many of the restaurant tables are in the high-ceilinged conservatory. Daniel provides game specialities in the winter and fish - direct from Billingsgate each day throughout the year. The menu features braised snails, warm Roquefort tart and crepes de fruit de mer gratinee. Those whose culinary horizons extend no further than Dover can choose oak-smoked salmon, roast Ayelsbury duck or the chef's venison casserole. Many customers come just for the food, and the Plough attracts many people from the National Trust attraction of Igtham Mote in the summer months. *The Plough, High Cross Road, Ivy Hatch, Sevenoaks, Kent TN15 0NL, Tel: 01732 810268*

Ightham
Map 1 ref D4
4 miles E of Sevenoaks on the A227

Ightham, pronounced *"item"*, is a lovely village in its own right even if many visitors are initially disappointed to learn that it is not the location of Ightham Mote. The core of the village is a group of half-timbered houses, and crooked lanes leading out. Just across the busy A25 is **Oldbury Hill**, an Iron Age hill fort covering roughly 150 acres on the top of a ridge.

Borough Green
Map 1 ref D4
4 miles E of Sevenoaks on the A25

Borough Green was only a small settlement before the arrival of the railway in the 19th century. This late - in comparison with some if its neighbours - development accounts for the lack of old buildings, although this small town does contain a number of fine examples of Victorian architecture, notably the Railway Hotel public house and a number of shop premises along the Maidstone Road.

A handy location - just five minutes' drive from the M20, M25 and M2 - gives **Fairseat House** a distinct advantage as a base for exploring Kent. And as it is only a 10 minute walk from the mainline station (London 40 minutes) this convivial B&B also attracts its share of rail travellers. The five rooms all have colour television and tea/coffee machines, while the public rooms have a breezy, flower-

Fairseat House

filled charm. Owner Gerald Bonham Thomas, a retired physicist, is an interesting and congenial host, and guests benefit from his acquaintance with local attractions such as Knole, Chartwell, Ightham Mote and Leeds Castle. Fairseat House is licensed and also serves home-cooked evening meals as well as hearty breakfasts. With the ports of Dover and Sheerness each just an hour's drive away, it also makes a good jumping-off point for a trip to the continent. The private car park makes staying at Fairseat House even more convenient. *Fairseat House, 100 Maidstone Road, Borough Green, Sevenoaks, Kent TN15 8HG, Tel: 01732 883975*

CHAPTER THREE
The Weald of Kent

Whitbread Hop Farm, Beltring

Chapter 3 - Area Covered

For precise location of places please refer to the colour maps found at the rear of the book.

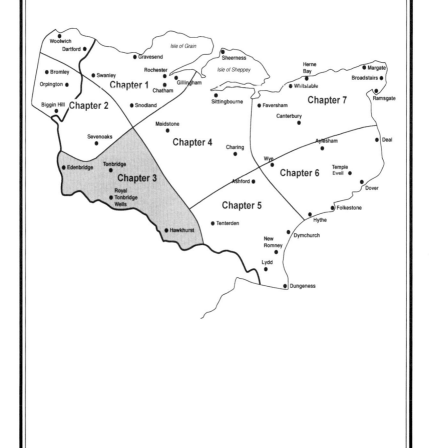

3
The Weald of Kent

Introduction

The Weald of Kent is a name to be reckoned with, one with many associations for anyone with imagination. It conjures up - quite accurately - images of rolling wooded countryside, orchards and hopfields.

Within this countryside there is much evidence of human habitation, whether it is in the form of Royal Tunbridge Wells, with its raffish sense of history, Tonbridge, commanding the heights over the Medway, or simply one of the dozens of villages that nestle among orchards or woods.

It is the balance between the natural and the man-made that is so harmonious here. Even the largest town, Royal Tunbridge Wells, owes its existence to the relatively recent discovery of its mineral springs. Tonbridge marks the highest navigable point of the Medway - again a natural justification for the siting of the town. And the villages themselves sometimes give a clue to their origins with their names. Even if the pronunciation of their names sometimes puzzle outsiders, there are often cues in the spelling. Most of these were carved from the forest in the Middle Ages or earlier. Those ending with *"hurst"* were built within the woods themselves, while those with the suffix *"den"* arose in the clearings. What is remarkable is that many villages seem to live up to the origins evoked by their names; the Weald remains one of the most consistently wooded areas of England and one that has preserved its traditions as well as its appearance.

Royal Tunbridge Wells

Royal Tunbridge Wells is the youngest of the centres that open the chapters of this book. Unlike Canterbury and Rochester, it can trace no Roman or ecclesiastical lineage. Sevenoaks to the north and Tenterden to the east can boast Medieval trading links but throughout the period during which these other towns were establishing their reputation Tunbridge Wells was nothing more than forest.

The secret of how this attractive town gained such prominence lies in the two words at the beginning and end of its name. First the *"wells"*. Until 1606, when Lord North discovered the chalybeate springs, this was an unremarkable tract of forest land. North, however, realised the importance of his discovery and rushed back to the court. That is where the second word, "Royal", comes in. Soon members of the Royal Family and courtiers were taking the waters, and spreading the word of their health-restoring qualities. For three decades there were no buildings by the springs. In 1630 Queen Henrietta Maria, the wife of Charles I, came here to recuperate after giving birth to the future Charles II. She and her retinue simply camped on the grounds by the springs. By the end of that decade, though, enterprising local people began building the town around the springs.

The town really came into its own in 1735 when Beau Nash, famous for his dominant role in Bath, arrived as Master of Ceremonies. With Nash at the helm, guiding and even dictating fashion, Tunbridge Wells went from strength to strength. Royalty was a constant factor in the following period, a fact that was officially recognised when Edward VII granted its *"Royal"* prefix in 1907.

Royal Tunbridge Wells is still a thriving town even if it no longer has the rakish atmos-

The Pantiles

phere of the 18th century. With visitors - and money - pouring in for two centuries the town acquired a prosperous look, which it has managed to retain with great charm. Nowhere is this more evident than in the **Pantiles**, a lovely shaded walk which is lined with elegant shops and overhung in places with an 18th century *"musick balcony"*. The Pantiles was originally grassed and known as The Walks. In 1699 Princess Anne visited Tunbridge Wells with her son, the Duke of Gloucester who slipped and hurt himself along The Walks. The irate Princess complained and the town authorities soon paved The Walk with square pantiles, and the name duly changed.

The Pantiles provides an appropriate setting for **Pantiles Spa Antiques**, one of the most respected antiques dealerships in a community that knows its antiques. Owner Janette Cowpland has been an antiques lover since childhood. Janette restored the present showroom location in 1990 and in doing so won an award from the Civic Society for Aesthetic Achievement. She specialises in excellent furniture, dining tables, boardroom tables, and sets of chairs. The

Pantiles Spa Antiques

showroom has specialist dealers in a wide-ranging selection of silver, silver plate, jewellery, Tunbridge ware, oil paintings, watercolours, prints, clocks, dolls, teddy bears, Art Deco and Art Nouveau, Arts and Crafts, and many other interesting items. The ample size of the showrooms allows these to be displayed in room settings. Pantiles Spa Antiques helps customers decide on shippers and will even deliver large items free within a range of 30 miles. *Pantiles Spa Antiques, 4/5/6 Union House, Pantiles, Royal Tunbridge Wells., Kent TN4 8HE Tel: 01892 5411377 Fax: 01435 865660*

The Pantiles were the focal point of the hectic social life organised by Beau Nash, and there were concerts, balls and gambling houses throughout the Season. People such as Sarah Porter, the *"Queen of the Touters"*, pestered strollers into entering the gambling halls. Only 15 of the original pantiles remain; these can be seen by the springs in Bath Square. The common extends down to the Pantiles, providing a sense of space and rural charm right in the heart of the town. It covers some 250 acres and is laced with gorse-lined footpaths along its grassy slopes. which also feature some curiously weathered rocks.

With town and country so evenly balanced, a visitor's bracing ramble can quickly evolve into a stroll past a row of fine old houses. Some of the best Regency architecture can be found along the gracefully curving *Calverley Park Crescent*. White-painted iron pillars support a covered promenade over a handsome terrace. Near it is *Calverley Grounds*, with rose gardens, shrubs, tennis courts and a paddling pool for children. Other fine Regency houses add lustre to the *Mount Sion* district.

Ideally suited as a walking base for the attractions of Royal Tunbridge Wells is *The Grove Tavern*, the oldest pub in this attractive town. The pub began life as a coaching inn and George, a coachman during that period, is said to haunt the pub. George is a friendly ghost, evidently, since he spends most of his time in the cellar, where the sound of clinking bottles usually announces his presence. Owners Paul and Julia Pinder, and their manager Grace Rhead, are the ideal people to approach with queries about the pub's racy history. They set the tone in a pub that relies more on its innate good cheer than

The Grove Tavern

any themed decor. Patrons drink at the single all-purpose bar, which has a wonderful full-length wooden floor. Hearty bar meals and snacks are available and there are four guest rooms for those who want to make the Grove Tavern their base for a walking tour of Tunbridge Wells. There is ample parking opposite. *The Grove Tavern, 34 Little Mount Sion, Tunbridge Wells, Kent TN1 1YS   Tel: 01892 526549*

The best place to learn about the history of Royal Tunbridge Wells is at the ***Tunbridge Wells Museum and Art Gallery,*** located in the Central Library in Mount Pleasant. It includes a fine selection of wooden souvenirs dating from the 17th century.

Western Woodlands

Rusthall
Map 1 ref D7

1 mile W of Royal Tunbridge Wells on the A264

Lying on the outskirts of Royal Tunbridge Wells, Rusthall just about manages to retain a sense of distinctiveness from its much larger neighbour. A lovely common marks the heart of Rusthall, emphasising its role as a community in its own right and not simply a suburb. Some of the unusual rock structures that feature in the common of Royal Tunbridge Wells crop up again in Rusthall. One of them, known as ***Toad Rock***, is a local landmark.

Few pubs can match ***The Mariners Rest*** for distinctiveness and the ability to live up to a name. The pub itself is a real find, blending in with its neighbours on a hilly residential lane. A patio to one side

The Mariners Rest

acts as a suntrap, luring customers outside even in early spring or late autumn. The interior, though, is the real talking point of this friendly free house. Decorating the walls of the small, cosy lounge are many photographs of the vessels which were skippered by Captain Heather Mitchell, co-owner of the Mariners Rest with her husband Alan. Heather and Alan spent many years operating trading vessels along the coastal and inland waterways of Holland, Belgium and northern France, and there are mementoes and anecdotes recalling those days. The Mariners Rest is only open evenings, although a knock or a telephone call has been known to open the doors of this fascinating pub in the afternoon. There is a small but appetising selection of food on request, and there is even a room available on a B&B basis. *The Mariners Rest, 6a Apsley Street, Rusthall, near Royal Tunbridge Wells, Kent TN4 8NU, Tel: 01892 5415541*

Much more than a country pub, **The Beacon** is a comfortable and relaxing home-from-home in a beautiful setting with genuinely helpful people on hand to make your meal go smoothly. In the winter guests can enjoy the welcome of a log fire while in the summer they can spread out on to the terrace and into the 16 acres of grounds, complete with lakes and woodlands. Appropriately set in Happy Valley, the Beacon is a friendly and informal bar with a reputation for good food and entertainment. The house itself dates back to 1895 and it was built as the country house of Sir Walter Harris, a former Lieutenant of the City of London. The dramatic

The Beacon

setting, with an outstanding view, combines with a spacious interior to make an ideal venue for receptions and other functions. Or it could prove to be the setting for the perfect murder - at one of the Murder Mystery Evenings, just one of the imaginative themed functions at the Beacon. *The Beacon Bar and Restaurant, Tea Garden Lane, Rusthall, near Royal Tunbridge Wells, Kent TN3 9JH, Tel: 01892 524252*

Set alongside the London to Brighton Coach Road in the village of Rusthall is **The Red Lion**, which was used by both Roundheads and Cavaliers in the English Civil War. It was first licensed in 1415 and it has seen more than its share of history, including a number of brushes with the authorities. Upstairs at this historic inn are the windows which were used to signal the warning and arrival of the Customs and Excise to the next pub across the valley. The Red Lion has an inglenook fireplace, with blazing fires throughout the winter, as well as many other features from the past. John and Joan

The Red Lion

Godden, the licensees, conjure up some imaginative speciality cooking as well as old favourites such as Spotted Dick pudding. The enormous garden is ideal for families and dogs are welcome provided they are kept under control. Visitors can also try their hand at some of the traditional pub games, perhaps taking on a local. The 17th century walled garden and medieval moat of Groombridge Place is nearby and Tunbridge Wells is only a coupe of minutes away by car. *The Red Lion, 82 Lower Green Road, Rusthall, Tunbridge Wells, Kent TN4 8TW Tel: 01892 520086*

Groombridge *Map1 ref C7*

5 miles W of Royal Tunbridge Wells off the A264

The village of Groombridge straddles the border between Kent and Sussex along the uplands that herald their nearness to the High Weald several miles south. The Kent side of the village is reckoned to be prettier and more interesting. In it visitors can find the triangular village green, which falls away from the tile-hung cottages that flank two of its sides with a decided slope. On the third side is **Groombridge Place**, which stands on the site of a former Norman castle. One of the best ways to approach Groombridge Place is along one of the paths that lead from the village; the path that sets off from the church offers some lovely views of the house as it enters its extensive grounds. Most of the structure visible today was built in the 17th century, very much in the style of Sir Christopher Wren. The gardens were designed by the famous Jacobean diarist John Evelyn and at the gates there is a small church - built as a private chapel by John Packer in 1625. A footpath continues through the grounds and then climbs above a stream, past another country estate - Homewood House - until it reaches the county boundary at High Rocks. There is a lovely backdrop of trees behind this outcrop, which makes an ideal setting for a picnic with a view.

Set just on a hill just outside the lovely village of Groombridge is **Ventura**, a comfortable and welcoming B&B run by Brenda and Cyril Horner. Guests feel immediately at home in the family-style surroundings, and the no-smoking rule makes Ventura even more attractive to anyone who values the clean country air. Rooms are light and airy, with sweeping views across the adjacent farms and

Ventura

woods. Guests eat in the sunny conservatory, which backs on to the extensive garden, which is well planted with flowers and attracts a variety of birds. Breakfast is a real treat, and the Horners provide home-baked bread, which can be spread with their own preserves. Ventura is popular with walkers and cyclists, which is not surprising since the house is well placed - a short walk to Groombridge in one direction and the public footpaths and walks leading in the other into the country. Locals rate Ventura highly, which is always a good recommendation, and it also has its share of repeat guests from Belgium, Holland and elsewhere on the Continent. *Ventura, The Ridge, Withyham Road, Groombridge, Kent TN3 9QU Tel: 01892 864711*

Speldhurst   Map 1 ref D6
4 miles NW of Royal Tunbridge Wells off the B2176

Speldhurst is one of the first villages west of Royal Tunbridge Wells to have a genuinely rural feel to it. It was mentioned as early as the 8th century and preserves a cohesive sense of village identity, centred on the church and the local pub. **Speldhurst church** stands where a much older Norman church had been built, the original having been struck by lightning in 1791. Great care was taken in the Victorian era to rebuild the church, and it is worth entering if only to see the stained-glass windows by Burne-Jones. Some pretty fields separate Speldhurst from the hamlet of Bullingstone Lane, which has a fascinating row of 15th century cottages.

Situated next to the old village church is **The George and Dragon**, a handsome pub that adds much to the charm of Speldhurst

The George and Dragon

Hill. The fine timbered entrance gives some indication of the pub's age, which has confidently been set at more than 700 years. It is even reputed to be the oldest building in Britain doing business as a public house. The main roofbeam support is made from the original timbers of one of Henry VIII's ships, and the inglenook fireplaces still have many marks left by knights sharpening their swords. Cara Baird has been chef since late 1997, but in that short time she has made her mark in the best possible way. Without sacrificing any of the "steeped in history" atmosphere of the pub she has set about establishing it as a beacon on the culinary map of Kent. Fresh ingredients, with an emphasis on fish, form the core of a menu that shows her flair and imagination, and complementing the large selection of wines and beers, including Harveys, Bass and Whitbread. *The George and Dragon, Speldhurst Hill, Speldhurst, Kent TN3 0NN Tel: 01892 863125*

Penshurst

Map 1 ref D6

5 miles NW of Royal Tunbridge Wells off the B2027

One of the prettiest villages in Kent is Penshurst, which makes the most of its hilly wooded setting and its Tudor architecture. The houses at its core are all old - dating from two to four centuries ago and each with its own sense of charm and identity.

A small and discreet "B&B" sign outside the handsome white clapboard *Village House* alerts guests that they have reached the end of their destination in the heart of this lovely village. And in some cases this welcoming establishment does represent the end of a real journey - owner Mrs Sally Warlow has regular guests from Australia and Japan. Slightly closer to home are the large numbers of Dutch guests, who know a good garden when they see one and flock to nearby Penshurst Place and its marvellous

The Village House

grounds. They - like all the guests at the Village House - appreciate Sally's friendliness and the bountiful breakfasts. Guests can feel like members of a select band - with only two guest rooms, the Village House retains a homely atmosphere. The old oak beams of the sitting room reinforce this cosy quality, but the effect in the house overall is light and airy. There are wonderful views from the rear of the house and local pubs and tea rooms are within easy walking distance. *The Village House, Penshurst, Kent TN11 8BT Tel/Fax: 01892 870234*

The heart of the village is the church of **Saint John the Baptist**, originally built in the 12th century and still containing elements from the 13th, 14th and 15th centuries. Of particular interest is the 15th century ornamental font. Almost as interesting as the church itself is the way it is reached - through an ancient lych-gate. The two-storey Tudor house which was built around the gate is now a test for geometry students, with its bulging walls and crooked beams hard-pressed to produce a right angle among them. Together with its neighbouring houses it makes up **Leicester Square**, although it would be hard to find a more tranquil counterpart to its namesake in the heart of the West End of London.

One of England's finest historic houses, **Penshurst Place** dominates the rural landscape of Penshurst and commands fine views over the Weald of Kent. The medieval house, renowned for its galleried Barons Hall, was built of local sandstone in 1341. Two centuries later it became the property of the Sidney family, who continued developing and adding to the estate. Today it stands as an impressive - and remarkably well-preserved - example of a defended manor house. A fascinating collection of armour, tapestries, paintings and furniture fills the state-rooms. Outside, there is the original ten-acre 16th century garden, the Toy Museum, a Venture Playground

Penshurst Place

and extensive walking trails. Penshurst Place can also claim England's second oldest cricket pitch. *Penshurst Place, Penshurst, Tonbridge Kent TN11 8DG, Tel: 01892 870307 Fax: 01892 870866*

With its creeper-clad walls and attractive gabled entrances, **The Leicester Arms** is generally numbered among the most picturesque inns in Kent. The Leicester Arms was once part of the estate of Penshurst Place, which had belonged to Sir William Sidney, grandfather of the Elizabethan poet Sir Philip Sidney. Another of Sir

The Leicester Arms

William's grandson's was appointed Earl of Leicester in 1618, and soon afterwards the inn was named in his honour. The seven bedrooms - including two four-poster rooms - in the hotel are comfortably and traditionally furnished as if in recognition of this distinguished pedigree. On the ground floor is the restaurant, which provides a wide ranges of dishes including fish and game; a bar menu offers lighter snacks. To the rear are lovely views of the rising meadowland through which the River Medway flows. Overseeing this delightful establishment are Chris and Sue Anscombe, who ensure that guests and diners make the most of their visit to the Leicester Arms. *The Leicester Arms, Penshurst, Kent TN11 8BT Tel: 01892 870551*

The 12 acre estate of **Penshurst Vineyards** capitalises on a south-facing situation and concentrates on five main varieties of grape. The result is an annual production that averages 40,000 bottles - the Penshurst wines are light and fruity, ranging from dry to

Penshurst Vineyards

medium. Apple wine and apple juice are also produced. Visitors are always welcome to look around and make purchases. Guided tours, which can be arranged by appointment, include a fuller explanation of viticulture and the equipment used in the production of high-quality wines. They end with a free tasting. There is also a chance to view some of the other residents of the Estate, who include a mob of wallabies and a flock rare sheep and exotic waterfowl. There is a picnic area and facilities for the disabled. *Penshurst Vineyards, Penshurst, Kent TN11 8DU, Tel: 01892 870255*

Chiddingstone   Map 1 ref C6
6 miles NW of Royal Tunbridge Wells off the B2027
The village of Chiddingstone is maintained by the National Trust and it is not hard to see why the Trust should be so interested in this small village set in pleasant open woodland roughly midway between Hever Castle and Penshurst Place. Chiddingstone grew prosperous in the 16th and 17th centuries and half-timbered houses from that period line the village's single street. The Trust has done an excellent job in supporting the preservation of these houses. They comprise a remarkable time-capsule of how the increased wealth from the Wealden iron industry transformed itself into a handsome and harmonious row of houses. The church predates the houses, having been built in the 13th century. It has a fine Gothic tower and handsome Jacobean font and pulpit.

At the head of the street, which in places is overhung by the upper storeys of the old houses, stands ***Chiddingstone Castle***. This is a mock-Gothic reworking of a much older house, the home of the Streatfield family. It contains a collection of Stuart furnishings and paintings as well as Ancient Egyptian and Oriental exhibits.

Along a footpath behind the street is a block of sandstone known as the Chiding Stone. Legend has it that in the distant past miscreants, vagrants and assorted petty criminals were taken here for a

Chiddingstone Village

public chastisement, or *"chiding"*. One wonders whether the dozens of individuals whose initials are carved in the rock faced an on-the-spot chiding.

A tiny lane beside the Castle Inn public house leads to ***Barbara Lane Antiques***, a small but well-stocked shop set in a charming Tudor cottage. Barbara and her family live on the opposite side of the lane, allowing her a certain flexibility in opening hours. The decidedly farm-like setting is deceptive - inside is a treasure trove of exquisite dinner services, delicate tables and chairs and a wealth of objets d'art. Displays benefit from being arranged to make the most of the natural light, which casts a warm glow on the dark parquet floor. This light, added to the quiet and Barbara's informative

Barbara Lane Antiques

but unobtrusive presence, draws customers into a feeling that they have walked into someone's comfortable sitting room. Barbara has been in the business for 30 years and she knows customers' needs, opening at unusual hours to cater to foreign visitors and able to suggest just the right gift or keepsake for anyone who asks. *Barbara Lane Antiques, Tudor Cottage, Chiddingstone, Edenbridge, Kent TN8 7AH,, Tel: 01892 870577*

Hever
Map 1 ref C6

13 miles W of Royal Tunbridge Wells off the B2026

The tiny village of Hever, near Edenbridge, is set in delightfully unspoilt countryside, with orchards and woodlands surrounding it. Most visitors, impressed as they may be with this tidy settlement, make for the star attraction here, and the reason why Hever figures prominently on anyone's checklist of things to see in Kent.

The village is the site of **Hever Castle**, which is redolent of history and more than a little tragedy. The castle achieved its present form in 1272 when Sir Stephen de Penchester received permission from Edward I to convert his house at Hever into a castle. The massive Gatehouse, the outer walls and the moat strengthened its position as a fortification.

Two centuries later the Bullen (or Boleyn) family bought the castle and rebuilt much of it, adding a comfortable Tudor residence inside the walls. It was here that the ill-fated Anne Boleyn, mother of Elizabeth I, was courted by Henry VIII. The castle still contains many mementoes of her. In 1903 Hever Castle was bought by American millionaire William Waldorf Astor, who restored the original buildings and set about building the *"Tudor Village"*, gardens and

Hever Castle

lake. All of these can be visited, as well as Hever Castle itself, with its fine collections of paintings, furniture and varied objets d'art. *Hever Castle, Hever, near Edenbridge, Kent TN8 7NG, Tel: 01732 865225*

Edenbridge
Map 1 ref C6

15 miles W of Royal Tunbridge Wells on the B2026

The village of Edenbridge, which lies near the Surrey border just north of the edge of the Weald, has been a settlement since Roman times. This is a Kentish place name which, although easy to pronounce, has a different twist to its tail. The etymology seems simple enough since there is a bridge here and it passes over the little river Eden. However, the bridge is actually named after a Saxon leader, Eadhelm, whose bridge replaced an earlier Roman one over the river. The name of the village settled easily into *"Edenbridge"*, and the river - unnamed in Eadhelm's time - became known as the Eden. Today's stone bridge is more recent still, dating from 1836. Edenbridge is a mixture of modern light industry and traces of former trade in iron and wool; one of the oldest buildings is **Doggetts Barn**, a tastefully restored example of traditional brick-and-timber architecture.

Along the Weald

Matfield
Map 2 ref E6

7 miles E of Royal Tunbridge Wells off the A21

Old and new houses blend harmoniously in the centre of Matfield, with its green and pond forming the heart of the village. The village green has the distinction of being one of the largest in Kent. Beside it are several fine tile-hung Kentish houses and an impressive Georgian. Just outside the village is another manor, **Crittenden House**, which has lovely gardens which are sometimes open to the public.

With a picturesque location by the village green, **The Wheelwrights Arms** makes an ideal spot to linger over a drink outside while a cricket match unfolds opposite on a long summer afternoon. This handsome white weatherboard pub was built in 1602 and was originally a farm building on a large estate. Through the centuries its role has changed, first as a grocery and bakery, then adding beer to the goods on offer in the mid-18th century. It assumed its present appearance around 1750 when it was first licensed as an ale house. On winter days, customers are met by a roaring log fire. Christine and Arthur Powell, the proprietors, are relatively recent arrivals,

The Wheelwright Arms

along with their three grown-up children who help in the bar and restaurant. Arthur enjoys sharing his newly acquired knowledge about the pub and its history, while Christine provides the home-baked gammons and other hearty fare that have customers coming back again and again. An interesting mix of patrons includes local villagers, cyclists, walkers and pilots from the local airport. Upstairs are five rooms which are available for B&B. *The Wheelwrights Arms, The Green, Matfield, Royal Tunbridge Wells, Kent TN12 7JX Tel: 01892 722129*

Narrow lanes lead south from Matfield, passing orchards and fields of hops. Mixed woodlands become thicker on the gently rising slopes as the road climbs to the next small village, ***Petteridge***.

Nestled among the orchards of Petteridge is ***The Hop Bine***, a traditional unspoilt country pub. As its name suggests, the Hop Bine lies in brewing country, and the pub takes its beer seriously. It is unique in being the only King & Barnes pub in Kent, serving their entire range of Sussex Ales. Hops also festoon the L-shaped bar and dried flowers brighten the disused cast-iron grate. A large double-sided fire blazes in winter and bench-seats fit along the half-panelled walls beneath old photographs of the building when it was two separate cottages. Michael and Beryl - or simply B - Winser ensure that customers enjoy themselves, and they provide some tasty home-cooked meals and bar snacks. Several tables and chairs about the

The Hop Bine

small lane to the front and there are picnic tables in the back garden. *The Hop Bine Inn, Petteridge Lane, Petteridge, Matfield, Kent
TN12 7NE, Tel: 01892 722561*

Horsmonden
12 miles E of Royal Tunbridge Wells on the B2162

Map 2 ref E6

The delightful village of Horsmonden (pronounced *"Horzm'den"*) was
once a thriving industrial centre, although it is hard to imagine now,
looking at the village tucked among smiling orchards and fields.
The key to this mystery lies in the pond that lies just west of the
village. Known as a furnace pond, it supplied the ironworks that
flourished along the Weald of Kent.

Today Nature seems to be reclaiming the pond, and soon it might
be indistinguishable from the other waterways in the meadows and
orchards around Horsmonden. Visitors - or worshippers - seeking
Horsmonden parish church have a chance to explore this countryside; the church lies 2 miles west of the village. A lovely footpath,
eventually leading to the church, sets off from the village green,
known as **The Heath**. The church contains a memorial to John Read
(d. 1847), the inventor of the stomach pump.

Standing amid rolling countryside and working farms is **Blackberry Barn**, which fits in naturally with its agricultural neighbours.
This remarkably modernised Grade II listed building, however, has
evolved from its farming role and now is a distinctive and impres-

Blackberry Barn

sive spot where paying guests are made to feel immediately at home. Simply to describe Blackberry Barn as a B&B would overlook its sense of style and the nature of the welcome provided by Mrs Diane Craft, its owner. The main area - of the barn - is open plan, with wooden floors, high ceilings, and a fine collection of paintings and objets d'art. Mrs Craft takes guests as and when she pleases, but those lucky enough to stay there feel like part of the family. The two guest rooms are lovingly decorated and have expansive views over the surrounding countryside. Many guests fall in with the sense of informality and have their breakfast in the snug kitchen although there is a well-appointed dining room. *Blackberry Barn, Spamonden Road, Horsmonden, Kent TN12 8EL Tel: 01580 211084*

Lamberhurst   *Map 2 ref E7*
10 miles E of Royal Tunbridge Wells on the A21
Lamberhurst lies on the main Royal Tunbridge Wells to Hastings road and its long high street follows the course of the road, crossing the river Teise. Many of the buildings and houses along this street are several centuries old, their trim well-maintained appearance reflecting the important role Lamberhurst once played as a coaching stop and as a centre of the iron industry.

There is a telling reminder of the past glories of Lamberhurst in the **parish church**, which is set some way from the centre of the village in the valley of the Teise. The interior of the church, which dates from the 14th century, has been remodelled to accommodate a smaller congregation - smaller, that is, than when Lamberhurst was central to the Wealden iron industry. Today viticulture is more important and there are several vineyards in the vicinity.

About a mile south-east of the village is **Scotney Castle**, a massive, rust-stained tower built in 1378 by Roger de Ashburnham. It incorporates the ruins of a Tudor house and is surrounded by a moat of water lilies set in lovely gardens. The gardens contain a wealth of plants, some of which have been grown in a disused quarry to give the effect of an Alpine garden.

About the same distance to the west of Lamberhurst is another romantic building, **The Owl House**, a tile-hung, half-timbered house built in the 16th century. Its remote location amid woodland lakes made it a popular haunt for wool smugglers although today it provides a tranquil welcome with its garden of fine spring flowers including azaleas, rhododendrons and rare shrubs.

Goudhurst
Map 2 ref F7

9 miles E of Royal Tunbridge Wells on the A262

Goudhurst, pronounced *"Gowdhurst"*, stands on a tall hill with sweeping views of the surrounding countryside of orchards and hopfields, and especially over the Weald to the north. The high street, which unfortunately can become choked with traffic in the summer, is lined with traditional Kentish tile-hung and weatherboard cottages. These are solid, well-built houses which reflect the prosperity that arose when the woollen industry was introduced in the Middle Ages. **St Mary's Church** stands at the top of the hill. Built mainly in the 15th century it shows English church architecture in transition with its mixture of Gothic and Renaissance styles. Inside there are many memorials to the leading local family, the Culpeppers.

Perched 400 feet above sea level in the Kentish Weald village of Goudhurst is **The Star and Eagle**, an inn with its roots in the Medieval period and which commands sweeping views of the surrounding orchards and hop gardens. Such a location would be the first choice for a hotel in this area, and the Star and Eagle can trace its origins back to the 14th century. Relics of vaulted stonework from that period are still visible in some parts of the building. During the 18th century the inn became the headquarters of the *"Hawkhurst Gang"* of robbers and smugglers. Nowadays things have quietened down considerably and guests are assured of a good night's sleep in one of the 11 bedrooms, each of which has its own character. Most have views either over the adjacent countryside or of the parish church. Downstairs are the restaurant and bars, with their exposed brickwork, ancient beams, and inglenook fireplace. Fine wines and locally brewed ales and beers complement an imaginative and wide-ranging menu. *The Star and Eagle, High Street, Goudhurst, Kent TN17 1AL Tel: 01580 211512*

The Star and Eagle

Just outside the village, downhill to the southwest, is **Finchcocks**, a Georgian red-brick mansion. Inside is an extensive historical musical collection which includes a number of early keyboard instruments. Further south, lying just east of the B2079, is **Bedgebury Pinetum**, which has the largest collection of conifers in Europe. Set in a natural wooded hillside it is a mixture of scientific nursery, museum of trees and a lovely parkland. The collection was begun in 1924 to grow experimentally various types of foreign trees, mainly conifers, which could not survive in the comparatively polluted atmosphere of Kew Gardens. Among the many species there are silver spruce, larches, cypresses and even some Californian redwoods.

Cranbrook
18 miles E of Royal Tunbridge Wells on the B2189

Map 2 ref F7

Cranbrook is an old town which sprang into prominence in the 15th century when it became a centre of the weaving industry. Several old buildings date back to this prosperous period and the winding streets, well away from any main road, are lined with weatherboarded shops and houses. The parish church, **St Dunstan's**, was built in the 15th century and is known locally as *"the Cathedral of the Weald"*. Above the porch is a room known as *"Baker's Jail"*, where *"Bloody Baker"* incarcerated the Protestants he had convicted before their execution.

The Union Mill, Cranbrook

Dominating the town, however, is the **Union Mill**, a three-storey windmill built in 1816. Standing 72 feet high it is the second tallest in England. It is open to the public at certain times of the year.

Sandhurst   *Map 2 ref G8*
19 miles SE of Royal Tunbridge Wells on the A268

Sandhurst lies on the southern fringes of Kent, set amid the orchards and hopfields of the Weald. This countryside accounts for the real attraction of the village, which is set on quite hilly terrain. This sloping landscape has given the name to a local pub, **The Missing Link**, which took its name from the habit of linking extra horses to wagons to pull loads up the hill. Sandhurst's parish church stands apart from the village itself, and has a fine view over the Kent Ditch into Sussex.

Those with a taste for wine and beer will find a visit to **Sandhurst Vineyards** fascinating. This working farm, run by the Nicholas family, offers a chance to see how grapes and hops are grown and harvested. Visitors can take well-marked farm walks ranging from 15 minutes to one hour, and they can watch the tradi-

Sandhurst Vineyards

tional hop picking in September. Most visitors finish with a free tasting and the chance to buy some of the award-winning wines. There are three rooms available for B & B in the 16th century farmhouse, which has comfortable accommodation and views over the hop farm. Dinners - featuring the Nicholases' own wine - are available by arrangement. *Sandhurst Vineyards and Hop Farm, Hoads Farm, Crouch Lane, Sandhurst, Cranbrook, Kent TN18 5PA Tel/Fax: 01580 850296*

North towards Maidstone

Tonbridge   *Map 1 ref D6*
5 miles N of Royal Tunbridge Wells on the A26
Tonbridge stands on the highest navigable point on the Medway and as such has been able to exploit this position over the centuries. There was an Anglo-Saxon settlement here and perhaps an earlier Roman community. Its most important historical landmark, on a rise in the centre of the town, is the ruined Norman ***castle***, of which there are substantial remains. The walls date from the 12th century while the shell of the keep, as well as the massive gatehouse and drum-towers, were built in the early 14th century. Inside the wall is a mound which is thought to have been the site of an Anglo-Saxon fort.

Tonbridge Castle

The parish **Church of Saints Peter and Paul** shows mainly evidence of the style of architecture known as Early English, in this case being built in the early 13th century. Subsequent restoration efforts and enlargements have altered the interior of the church, but it retains a sense of height and airiness that recalls the Middle Ages.

Tonbridge School was founded in 1553 by Sir Andrew Judd, Master of the Skinners' Company and former Lord Mayor of London, and received a charter from Elizabeth I. On Judd's death the administration was left in trust to the Skinners" Company, which have remained Governors to this day. The school is mainly housed in 19th century buildings in the High Street. The High Street leads north before a left turning on the B245 makes its way through the suburb of Hildenborough to make a rural alternative to the A21 towards Sevenoaks.

Standing proudly amid ten acres of well-maintained gardens is **The Plough Inn**, which provides a rural oasis just five minutes from the A21. Co-owners Sean McCorry and Kyla Scougall have run the Plough Inn for five years as a family business. Three chefs conjure up a varied menu which touches several international bases - including Toast Beverly Hills, Tiger Prawns and Pallo Pasta - but also stays true to its British roots with Shrewsbury Lamb, Pot Roast Pheasant and Steak and Ale Pie. Large parties are catered for in the Barn, a 16th century Elizabethan barn featuring the original beams. The restaurant, which seats around 40 people, is in the main

The Plough Inn

building with the bar itself. The low beams and parquet floors of the main bar area flank the small leaded windows which have been stained with the smoke of countless log fires. The atmosphere - complete with the touch of the exotic in the form of the resident iguana - is enticing, and there are two guest rooms providing bed and breakfast. *The Plough Inn, Powder Mill Lane, Hildenborough, Kent TN11 9AJ, Tel: 01732 832149*

Beltring   *Map 2 ref E6*
11 miles NE of Royal Tunbridge Wells off the B2106

Beltring is a trim little village which can boast a major Kent attraction, the **Whitbread Hop Farm**. Originally a hop-drying centre to supply the major brewery, this agricultural complex has grown to

Whitbread Hop Farm

house a museum, a crafts exhibition and a nature trail. Families make a day of a visit here, and children are well received, but it is easy to lose the original purpose of the farm. Visitors can learn a great deal about the brewing industry, its Kentish connections, and the purpose and history of hops in the renewing process. Until the 14th century, for example, cloves were more commonly used as flavouring.

Beer is the talking point at *The Blue Bell* in the village of Beltring - and for good reason. This charming pub, with its wavy old white wooden cladding and attractive gables, is flanked by an oast house and stands opposite the Whitbread Hop Farm. The famous Whitbread shire Horses can be seen from the picnic tables outside the Blue Bell, and patrons can soak in the bucolic atmosphere in what amounts to a pleasant sun trap. Inside, the Blue Bell is everything an old-fashioned English pub should be, with the agricultural

The Blue Bell

theme of its decor, the open fires, and the evocative old photographs of both pub and village. Despite the undeniable "beer" atmosphere of the setting, the Blue Bell also offers a lively choice of wines to complement a menu that ranges from soups and salads to hearty main courses that also cater to vegetarians. A choice of liqueur coffees adds an unashamedly hedonistic touch. *The Blue Bell, Beltring, near East Peckham, Kent TN12 6QH Tel: 01622 871496*

East Peckham
Map 2 ref E5

12 miles NE of Royal Tunbridge Wells off the B2106

East Peckham is a large village that stands on the banks of the Medway, surrounded by the rich farms that are given over to hops and the occasional orchard. East Peckham's ancient church is more than 2 miles from the village itself. It stands, disused now, in an isolated setting which now sees more bird-watchers - skylarks are still common here - than worshippers.

Set in thise *"Heart of Kent"* village is **The Harp**, a pub that has provided this rural community with good beer and good cheer for generations. The setting, in the centre of hop-picking country, couldn't be more appropriate for a pub that prides itself in an excellent selection of real ales - the end-product of the hop-pickers' labours. This is a pub in the true mould of the English village pub, with good talk, friendly hosts (and ghosts), open fires, and best of all, no pool

The Harp

tables or fruit machines. Every space inside the pub is filled with bric-a-brac and memorabilia, with a special emphasis on a wide-ranging collection of musical instruments which includes bagpipes, zithers, xylophones, a hunting horn, and even a digeridoo. There are good home-cooked meals, with Sunday lunch a popular favourite with locals and visitors alike. Tricia and James Chapman are hospitable and extrovert hosts who contribute to the family atmosphere of the pub. Patrons can savour the rural feel outside in the large garden with its picnic tables in warmer weather. *The Harp, Hale Street, East Peckham, Kent TN12 5JB Tel: 01622 872334*

Laddingford   *Map 2 ref E5*
13 miles NE of Royal Tunbridge Wells on the B2162
Laddingford is a small village, not much more than a hamlet, which lies in the heart of Orchard country. Tributaries of the Medway flow

south through this fertile agricultural landscape - this settlement grew out of one of the several fords passable throughout the year. From the heart of the village one can see orchards in nearly every direction, but looking south the wooded ridge, with Goudhurst at its crest, is clearly visible.

Acting as a hub for the village of Laddingford is *The Chequers*, a traditional pub that has a well-earned reputation for its convivial and welcoming atmosphere. Tracey and Charles Leaver run the pub with imagination and flair. Tracey is passionate about her flowers, and most people's first impression is formed by the profusion of colour to the front of the pub, no matter what time of year. To the rear are huge gardens, which act as a magnet for children. In addition to an *"assault course"* type of play area there is another section set aside for animals; children can feed the goats and rabbits under adult supervision.

The Chequers

Grown-ups needn't feel overlooked at the Chequers, and the interior comprises three areas all served by one large bar. Diners mingle with those who have simply stopped for a drink, and the clientele represents a lovely cross-section of Laddingford society. People constantly come and go, greeting Tracey and Charles on their way, adding to the sense that the pub serves a valuable function for the village. Newcomers are often drawn into conversations with locals. The food is traditional, no-frills pub grub, with daily specials featuring among the home-cooked selection.

The patio acts as overspill in the warmer weather and patrons can never be sure of what type of home-grown entertainment might meet them there. Perhaps it will be Morris Dancing, or maybe one of the pub's periodic beer festivals, or it might be one of the Chequers' offbeat charity fund-raising functions such as judging the biggest marrow in the village. All in all a visit to the Chequers is a welcoming and cheerfully unpredictable experience. *The Chequers, Laddingford, Maidstone, Kent ME18 6BP Tel: 01622 871266*

Yalding   *Map 2 ref E5*
14 miles NE of Royal Tunbridge Wells on the B2010

Another lovely village in the heart of Kent's orchard country, Yalding stands at the junction of the Medway, Beult and Teise rivers. This confluence provides ample irrigation for the fertile soil so it is not surprising that Yalding is actually the largest hop-growing parish in Kent. An ancient long narrow bridge crosses two of the rivers, linking the two halves of the village. A delightfully small high street climbs past weatherboard houses through the village, passing the parish church, with its onion dome slightly askew on the church tower.

Hadlow   *Map 1 ref E5*
11 miles N of Royal Tunbridge Wells on the A26

Hadlow lies in the Medway Valley within easy reach of Tonbridge. It is an attractive village with a wide main street and a number of old houses in the centre. These, however, are dwarfed by the main feature of Hadlow, a curiosity known as **Hadlow Tower**, or May's Folly. This 170 foot high tower is all that remains of Hadlow Castle, which an eccentric industrialist named Walter Barton May had built at the end of the 18th century. The folly is aptly named on two counts. First it represents the typical *"Gothick"* style of architecture so dear to the Romantic era, when defiantly non-utilitarian follies were the rage. Second, it was reputedly built so that May could have a view as far as the Channel, but the intervening South Downs make this impossible.

West Peckham   *Map 1 ref E5*
12 miles N of Royal Tunbridge Wells off the A26

West Peckham is a quiet village in the midst of smiling orchard country, with fields surrounding the village and no main roads running through the most attractive parts of it. The parish church of St Dunstan lies down a narrow lane and stands opposite the village green. The church predates the Norman Conquest and there are some fascinating wooden carvings behind the altar - although these seem to be of a later date.

West Peckham is on the Wealdway and Greensand Way footpaths, which trace their way across the higher ground in the vicinity. Another footpath, leading west from the village, passes the edge of **Oxen Hoath**, a large mansion and estate built by the Culpepper family. Further along the path, from a stone bridge by a small lake, there is a good view of the house, which commands excellent views of the Medway Valley and the Weald.

Nettlestead   Map 1 ref E5
13 miles N of Royal Tunbridge Wells on the B2015

Nettlestead is a quiet village set on a bank above the Medway. The two reasons for visiting this small village are its parish church and the manor house. **Nettlestead Church** lies between the cricket pitch and the river. It dates from the late 15th century and has lovely stained glass windows, which were severely damaged in 1763 when a thunderstorm unleashed 10-inch hailstones on the village.

Next to the church is **Nettlestead Place**, a private home which contains an undercroft built in the 13th century.

Mereworth   Map 1 ref E5
13 miles N of Royal Tunbridge Wells on the A228

Mereworth is something of a curiosity. Early in the 18th century a local landowner, John Fane, built a Palladian mansion here. He was quickly disappointed, however, not because of the house itself but because the local village blocked some of its view of the adjacent countryside. Fane had the offending village demolished and replaced with a new one nearby, but out of the line of sight from his own home. The new village had houses for all its inhabitants and Fane even had a new church built. This being the 1740's, the church architecture owed a lot to Sir Christopher Wren, whose churches still grace the London skyline. The result was a faithful facsimile of Saint Martin in the Fields.

CHAPTER FOUR
From Maidstone to the Sea

Interior, Boughton Monchelsea Place

Chapter 4 - Area Covered

For precise location of places please refer to the colour maps found at the rear of the book.

4

From Maidstone to the sea

Introduction

Rivers, woodlands and sea play an important role in forming the landscape and character of Kent, and the area stretching from the county seat, Maidstone, eastwards has all of these in abundance. As with other parts of Kent, the modern appearance of towns and villages reflects how these elements fused together organically, and how the final *"human"* layer is simply a thin veneer.

Even a few paces from the busy and at times traffic-choked streets of Maidstone there are tranquil riverside scenes, particularly in the stretch of the Medway by the former Archbishops Palace. It is in redeveloped areas such as this that enlightened modern planners have returned to their roots, so to speak, in finding the reason why a settlement developed and then doing their best to restore it. Similar thinking has gone into the well-planned traffic bypasses which have spared - or even revived - the centres of towns and villages such as West Malling and Detling.

Maidstone, as well as being strategically located along the Medway, lies between the Weald of Kent and the North Downs. The orchard country around the county seat gradually gives way to more wooded uplands of the downs as one moves east. Sittingbourne, on the far side of the Downs, is the gateway to the Isle of Sheppey, which includes not only one of Britain's most important ferry ports (Sheerness) but also coastal levels and beaches to attract bird-watchers, yachtsmen and swimmers. And in Minster it contains an Abbey with a fascinating history.

Maidstone

Maidstone developed on the site of an important meeting place. The name means *"the people's stone"*, and it is likely that a stone marked the site of the *"moot"*. The River Medway is the ancient boundary which separated West and East Kent, and Maidstone was once the capital of the former. On the west of the river lived the *"Kentish Men"*, while to the east lived the *"Men of Kent"*. The distinction is still used proudly by many of the inhabitants of the county today.

Although Maidstone has been extensively developed in recent years, there are several handsome Elizabethan and Georgian buildings to be found hidden away in the High Street and surrounding backstreets. Maidstone's **Museum and Art Gallery** is housed in the beautiful Chillington Manor House, a splendid Tudor residence which is in St Faith's Street. In the Museum is a chair from nearby **Allington Castle** which bears a fascinating inscription. Henry VIII is said to have first met Anne Boleyn at Allington, and the chair is a fitting testimony to this man who loved women. The motto reads: *".of this (chay)re iss entytled too one salute from everie ladie thott settes downe in itt - Castell Alynton 1530 - Hen. 8 Rex"*. Which, loosely translated, means that gallant Henry could demand a kiss from every woman fortunate (or possibly foolhardy) enough to sit on it!

For another unusual glimpse of the past, you should make your way to the Stables of the former **Archbishop's Palace** in Mill Street. Close to here you will find a wonderful exhibition of horse-drawn carriages, The **Tyrwhitt-Drake Museum**. This grand mixture of private and State carriages makes up one of the finest collections of its kind in England.

Kent plays county cricket in **Mote Park**, to the east of the town, an extensive area of 450 acres of parkland with fishing and sailing on a lake formed by damming the River Len.

Around Maidstone

Aylesford *Map 2 ref F4*
2 miles N of Maidstone on the A229
Just north of Maidstone is the picturesque village of Aylesford. Having travelled these many miles from Pegwell Bay, the Jutish leaders Hengist and Horsa vanquished the ancient Britons at Aylesford in a great battle in AD455. This was frankly unsporting of them, having been invited into Britain by the British ruler Vortigern

to help him defend the country from his enemies! Horsa died in the battle, leaving Hengist and his son Aesc to establish the kingdom of the Cantware, or *"men of Kent"*. For 300 years, the kingdom was ruled by the descendants of Aesc - the dynasty of the Eskings.

In Aylesford's High Street is the splendid medieval *Friary* built by the Carmelites around the middle of the 13th century. This was the first Carmelite order to be founded in Europe. Following the Dissolution, the Friary was rebuilt in 1675, but the main part of the house was destroyed by fire in the 1930's. The Carmelites took over the house in 1949 and have successfully restored it to its former glory.

Aylesford exudes history and charm as it sits demurely on the banks of the Medway. As an important river crossing, it has seen a great deal of activity throughout the centuries. A beautiful five-arched *medieval bridge* spans the river, and the surrounding jumble of timbered and gabled dwellings ensures that many visitors stop to muse for a while. It is not surprising that countless photographers and painters, both professional and not so professional, have eagerly attempted to capture the tranquil beauty of Aylesford over the years.

Boxley   *Map 2 ref F4*
2 miles N of Maidstone off the A249

The village of Boxley is a little gem which deserves *"hidden"* status given its close proximity to Maidstone as well as the M2 and M20 motorways. It has a lucky position, tucked in woodland on the edge of the North Downs. Just outside the village, to the west, are the ruins of *Boxley Abbey*, within sight of the North Downs Way, which passes by along a hillside to the north.

An inn since 1545, when Henry VIII first registered it as an ale house, *The King's Arms* in Boxley can trace its history back some 350 years further. It was built as a monk's hostelry in 1195 during the reign of Richard I and its sign displays the arms of Richard II, who visited Boxley in 1381. The site was chosen because it was opposite the church of St Mary's All Saints; Boxley Abbey itself is about one mile southwest. The pub lives up to its illustrious history with its magnificent interior. Oak panelling abounds and there are leather armchairs and a huge inglenook fireplace with blazing log fires. The King's Arms is noted for its good range of cask ales, numbering about 15, and the diverse wine list features many representatives from the New World as well as Continental vineyards. Manager Helen Sutton also presides over the dining at the

The King's Arms

King's Arms, which offers a full range of meals and snacks. The spacious garden has some good views of the surrounding rolling countryside. *The King's Arms, Boxley, near Maidstone, Kent ME14 3DR Tel: 01622 755177*

Detling
3 miles NE of Maidstone off the A249

Map 2 ref F4

Detling once served as an important coaching stop on several major routes linking Maidstone with Sittingbourne, Faversham and other towns to the north. The high street, which had been the main thoroughfare for these coaches, is now a more tranquil street, its role having been taken by the A249 which lies just to the north of the village. Pretty cottages are dotted through the village which lies on the south-facing slopes of the North Downs.

A sloping corner location is a clue to the name of **The Cockhorse Inn**, in the village of Detling near Maidstone. Its address, The Street, was once the main Maidstone to Sittingbourne road and the pub began as a coaching inn. Its original name was the Cock, but this changed in honour of the inn's heavy horses, which helped lighter horses with their carriages up the steep hill. Inside this snug and cosy pub it is easy to imagine cold and weary travellers warming

The Cockhorse Inn

themselves by the double-sided open fire while they had a meal or drank some ale. Entering the pub, visitors get a sense of its being quite small, but this feeling is dispelled as they venture further and further back until they reach the huge inglenook fireplace and big log fire. Oak beams and bare brick walls contribute to the sense of the past, and old photographs and pictures trace the pub's coaching inn past. There is a good range of cask beers and the extensive menu features a house speciality - a huge steak and kidney pie weighing one pound. *The Cockhorse Inn, 39 The Street, Detling, near Maidstone ME14 3JT Tel: 01622 737092*

West Malling   *Map 2 ref E4*
5 miles W of Maidstone on the A20

A recent bypass has spared the centre of West Malling from the worst excesses of traffic problems. This enlightened move has left its wide high street - and the Georgian houses that line it - better able to present its handsome face to the outside world. There is a feeling of West Malling's being larger than a village and indeed it was once called Town Malling. It certainly has more history than most villages could absorb.

An Anglican Abbey for nuns (in Swan Street) and a monastery in Water Street carry on traditions dating from the 11th century when William the Conqueror's bishop Gundulph founded the abbey. He also built **St Leonard's Tower**, the ruined keep of the house in which he lived. The tower stands by the entrance to **Manor Park**

Country Park, which comprises 52 acres of parkland and an ornamental lake.

A handy location right in the high street of West Malling makes **The Joiners Arms** an ideal base for exploring this lovely traditional village. The pub, with its bow-windowed front and steep tiled roof, is very much in keeping with the old-fashioned architecture of the village. That is not surprising, since this building has been a village pub for all of its 300 year history. Inside there are two old-style bars, one carpeted and the other with a plain wooden floor. In the *"back"* room the wood-panelled walls and 18th century fireplace

The Joiners Arms

simply exude atmosphere, while the "front" bar offers patrons the chance to gaze out on passers-by along the high street while seated by an open fire. There is a separate eating area at the rear of the pub, beyond which is a beer garden. Owners Derren and Rebecca Howells are an energetic and lively young couple who extend their normal pub food menu to mark special occasions such as Valentines Day and Mothers Day. *The Joiner Arms, 64 The High Street, West Malling, Kent ME19 6LU   Tel: 01732 840723*

People looking for a pampered overnight stay in lovely surroundings should make for **Blacklands House**, an elegant Georgian residence in a quiet hamlet only 4 miles from Maidstone. Built in 1830 for a local mill owner and gentleman farmer, the house stands

Blacklands House

in attractive gardens with a stream, lake and waterfall nearby. Blacklands House retains many of its original features and the floor-to-ceiling french windows on the ground floor make the interior light and airy. Chandeliers and other furnishings reflect the origins of the house, which has its original shutters still in place and an imposing archway in the dining room. The five guest rooms are spacious and full of character. Owner Ann Leonard takes great pride in both the house and the way in which guests return time and again to her appealing house.   *Blacklands House, Blacklands, East Malling, near Maidstone, Kent ME19 6DS Tel: 01732 844274*

Offham   *Map 2 ref E4*
6 miles W of Maidstone on the A228
Offham, a lovely small village set in the orchards of the North Downs, was first settled by the Romans. Its main conversation piece today, however, is of slightly more recent vintage. In the middle of the attractive village green is a *quintain*, or tilting post. This aid for jousting practice consists of an upright with an arm that swivels when hit - particularly by a lance. The quintain comes into play each year during Offham's May Day celebrations.

Barming   *Map 2 ref F5*
4 miles W of Maidstone on the A26
Barming is a predominantly residential area that has been subsumed into Maidstone and so bears little resemblance to the original village. However, it does possess a lovely wooden bridge over the Medway, which provides a starting point for a choice of riverside

walks. One such walk goes to East Farleigh, hugging the river bank while steep hills rise to the south.

East Farleigh

Map 2 ref F5

2 miles SW of Maidstone on the B2010

East Farleigh stands among the orchards of the Medway Valley. The village itself is high above the river but there is a fine ***medieval bridge*** crossing it below. Dating from the late 15th century, the bridge spans the 100 yard-wide Medway in five graceful arches. Cromwell's New Model Army, under Fairfax, crossed this bridge in 1648 to take Maidstone in one of the most important engagements of the Civil War. The battle left 300 Royalists dead and more than a thousand taken prisoner. The bridge is now a national monument.

Located right in the heart of the lovely village of East Farleigh, ***The Bull*** is a popular pub that has been refreshing travellers and locals alike since the days of coaching inns. There is a graphic reminder of that era in front of the pub, where a time-worn mounting block gives mute testimony to centuries of use beneath the huge

The Bull

chestnut tree. East Farleigh church stands just opposite and to the rear of the Bull is a huge beer garden which commands lovely views from its elevated position. Inside, there is an open-plan bar and dining area with wood-panelled walls decorated with old photographs, converted gaslights and oil lamps, and lines of books. There is a good choice of food, including barbecue choices outside in the summer. Parents can enjoy a quiet drink or meal outside while the children meet Winston, the pot-bellied pig and star of the animal farm which also includes chickens, geese, and rabbits. *The Bull, Lower Road, East Farleigh, Maidstone, Kent ME15 0HD Tel: 01622 726282*

Benefiting from a lovely position - high on an elevated site overlooking the river - is ***The Victory***, a popular pub which attracts a good number of sailors in addition to a loyal local following. A large

beer garden makes the best use of both available space and location, as it looks back down on the river. A hundred people can be seated here comfortably and in the summer there are barbecues and special pay areas for children. The inside of this free house is no disappointment: there are three separate areas each with its own snack bar. Brickfaced fireplaces offer cheery warmth in two of the bars and the snug bar features some original bar billiards. Publican Mike Kidner has been in the trade for 30 years and presides over a selection of three lagers, four bitters, and four real ales. The food has also earned the Victory a good reputation, with home-cooked choices ranging from bar snacks to a full a la carte menu in the new restaurant section. *The Victory, Farleigh Bridge, East Farleigh, Maidstone, Kent ME16 9NB Tel: 01622 726591*

The Victory

Loose   Map 2 ref F5
2 miles S of Maidstone off the B2010

Pronounced *"Looze"*, this village has been fighting a partly losing battle to preserve its identity in the face of expansion from Maidstone. The older part of the village lies in a narrow little valley, where millponds once powered a flourishing woollen industry. When the wool trade declined the mills were converted to paper-making. This change signalled more contact with Maidstone, which has gradually absorbed the northern fringe of the village into its outskirts. **The Wool House**, located just off the A229, is a National Trust-owned property which traces the story of the wool trade in Loose.

Otham   Map 2 ref F5
3 miles SE of Maidstone off the A2

The lovely village of Otham is a haven of tranquillity despite being so close to Maidstone. It is set in orchard country and the solid yeomen's houses in the heart of the village reflect the farming prosperity over the centuries. An excellent example of this architecture is Stoneacre, which was built near the end of the 15th century. It is open to the public at stated times throughout the year.

Leeds   Map 2 ref G5
4 miles SE of Maidstone off the A2

The village of Leeds stands on the grounds of a former Abbey, which flourished until the Dissolution in the 16th century. Many of the older features of the village, such as its oast-houses, Norman church and surrounding farms, were part of the Abbey complex.

Climbing flowers frame the handsome double bow windows that welcome visitors to **West Forge**, which offers B&B accommodation in the village of Leeds. The Wiesbauers, who own West Forge, are an international couple - he is Austrian and she is English - and between them they speak German, Spanish, and French as well as English. They provide a welcoming and relaxed atmosphere while offering all sorts of maps, leaflets, and other information for people touring the area. Children are made especially welcome: cots are available and there is a climbing frame in the large gardens. In the last century the building was indeed a forge, and traces of this blacksmithing history are also outside in the gardens. Guests enjoy a real sense of privacy, with a separate front door and their own keys. Evening meals are available on request. *West Forge, Back Street, Leeds, near Maidstone, Kent ME17 1TF Tel: 01622 861 428*

West Forge

The feature that dominates the village, however, is **Leeds Castle**, which stands on two islands in the middle of the River Len. This peaceful moat is the home of swans and ducks, and surrounding the castle are the extensive gardens laid out by Capability Brown in the 18th century. The present castle structure, with its romantic turrets and stout walls, dates from the time of Edward I although there has been a defensive fortress on the site since the middle of the 9th century. It was Henry VIII who effected the transformation from a strategically sited fortress into a stately country residence. For 300 years it remained a royal residence, with additions, such as the main building, designed to blend harmoniously with the rest of the complex. Today it is open to the public and one of the most popular

Leeds Castle

attractions in Kent if not all of the South East. Even when thronged with visitors and surrounded by coaches Leeds Castle exudes an air of timeless charm, with the mature oaks and horse chestnuts in its grounds seeming to frame the castle itself.

Leeds also is the heart of a countryside district of hidden and attractive hamlets, some of which seem to be organic elements of the woodlands that still cover much of the area.

By turning off the main A20 just 2 miles south of Maidstone and following signs for Weavering Street, thirsty travellers can trace their way to **The Fox and Goose**, an old-style local pub with a friendly atmosphere. Proprietors Colin and Barbara set the cheerful tone; Colin - a self-confessed golf fanatic - has photographs and other memorabilia from various tournaments. Barbara served on the Board of the Licensed Victuallers Governors for 15 years, so it is

The Fox and Goose

not surprising that the pub is well run. There are two bars inside providing both Courage and various *"guest ales"*, all of which are hand-pumped and in top condition. Good-value food can be eaten in the large dining area and the pub is flanked by both a large beer garden and a huge car park. *The Fox and Goose, Weavering Street, Weavering, Maidstone, Kent ME14 5JP Tel: 01622 737675*

South of Maidstone

Chart Sutton and Sutton Valence   *Map 2 ref G5*
5 miles SE of Maidstone on the A274

The centre of Chart Sutton lies just off the main Maidstone to Tenterden road, and the village grew in previous centuries in order to cater to the passing trade. Today's village, however, has reverted to a more agricultural setting, and it is surrounded by large farms which extend up the hills. Footpaths leading west from the village centre climb some of these hills, from which there are fine views looking out past Boughton Monchelsea - only a couple of miles away - and further towards Maidstone.

Travellers in the vicinity of Maidstone who are looking for a traditional experience should beat a path to *White House Farm*, located in the village of Chart Sutton just south of Maidstone. Benefiting from a quiet rural setting just outside the village, this is a working farm which offers comfortable B&B accommodation. The house itself is a traditional wood-framed building with an unusually large chimney. Inside it is everything that a farmhouse should be, with its low exposed beams, uneven floors, and blazing fires. Mrs Susan Spain, the owner, has managed to convey the feel of living in a real farmhouse for her guests, who have their own breakfast/dining/sitting room. Both of the guest bedrooms are full of charac-

White House Farm

ter, and the only sounds are those provided by the farm animals. Evening meals are sometimes available by prior arrangement. *White House Farm, Green Lane, Chart Sutton, Maidstone, Kent ME17 3ES Tel/Fax: 01622 842490*

Sutton Valence enjoys a hilltop setting with lovely views of the surrounding countryside. There are ruins of an old castle, a grammar school of great antiquity, and in the parish church there is a monument to John Willes, who introduced round-armed bowling to the sport of cricket.

Easily reached along the A274, **Sutton Valence Antiques** is just a couple of minutes' walk from the centre of this charming village. This family-run business was founded 20 years ago and has grown to be the largest of its kind in Kent. The shop comprises an old timbered cottage along with some later Victorian buildings and

Sutton Valence Antiques

there is parking on site and nearby. There are marvellous views over the Weald of Kent. Sutton Valence Antiques carries a wide range of stock both at the shop itself and at the warehouse nearby. Although people from around the world come to buy, casual browsers are always welcome to ramble from room to room enjoying a step into the past. *Sutton Valence Antiques, Sutton Valence, near Maidstone, Kent ME17 3AP Tel: 01622 843333, Fax: 01622 843499*

Boughton Monchelsea
Map 2 ref F5

6 miles S of Maidstone off the B2163

As the centre of Kentish ragstone quarrying it is not surprising that the centre of this pleasant village reflects the local building material. The **quarries**, on the edge of the village, have been worked almost continuously for seven centuries but archaeologists suggest that they were used much before since both the Romans and the Saxons used the stone. Some of these stones were used in the building of Westminster Abbey and Henry III ordered a number of cannonballs to be made from the stone. The parish church, **St Peter's**, was built from ragstone in the Norman period. The lych-gate,

Boughton Monchelsea Place

erected in 1470, was built entirely without nails and is thought to be the oldest in England.

The manor house, **Boughton Monchelsea Place**, is another ragstone building. It was the home of Sir Thomas Wyatt who led the Men of Kent in revolt against Mary I and was executed in 1554. The present manor house dates from shortly after this but was extensively remodelled in the 18tth century. The house and its extensive gardens are open to the public.

Staplehurst
Map 2 ref F6

9 miles S of Maidstone on the A229

There was once a stronghold here, but today all that can be seen is a tree-covered mound, and nobody seems quite certain as to who built the fortification. It is however worth a visit as it is home to a rather interesting place where you can step back in time and wander through beautiful gardens where the air is filled with delicate perfumes and all is peaceful.

A trail of brown tourist signs with a white flower emblem leads from the centre of Staplehurst village to **Iden Croft Herbs**, which specialises in culinary, aromatic and medicinal herbs. This is not simply an outlet for the herbs - they are grown in tranquil gardens along with alpines, wildflowers, herbaceous plants and species that attract bees and butterflies. A series of paths wander through gardens of varying sizes until they reach the main attraction, a 15th century walled garden. Here is where visitors can be reminded of less stressful times, while being reminded that natural aromatherapy has a much longer history than they might have thought. There are many seats throughout the gardens, and gardeners will find seeds and plants on sale

Iden Croft Herbs

in the shop, where there are also light refreshments. *Iden Croft Herbs, Frittenden Road, Staplehurst, Kent TN12 0DH Tel: 01580 891432 Fax: 01580 892416, E-mail: idencroft.herbs@dial.pipex.com*

Headcorn
Map 2 ref G6

9 miles S of Maidstone on the A274

Headcorn was once a major cloth-making centre and the **Cloth Hall** which reflects this former source of prosperity. The parish church has a lovely location right at the end of the main street. Behind it is **Headcorn Manor**, a 16th century hall house which is fronted by a two-storey oriel window. Just a few miles south of the village, at Lashenden, is the RAF Association's **Museum of Air Warfare**, which commemorates the role played by this corner of the South East during the Battle of Britain and throughout the Second World War.

Golf and outdoor pursuits are the big attractions at **Weald of Kent**, an attractive golf course offering a chance to savour the beau-

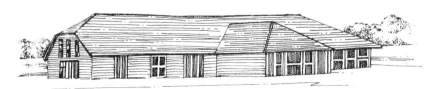

The Weald of Kent

tiful Kent countryside, yet within easy reach of Maidstone, Ashford, Tunbridge Wells, and the Medway towns. Non-members are welcome to tackle the 6,169 yard, par 70 course, which tests players with its ditches, gullies, undulating fairways, and natural water hazards. Buggies are available in dry weather and the well-stocked golf shop stocks a wide range of equipment and clothing. But there is more to Weald of Kent than simply golf, as a visit to the welcoming bar proves. A value-for-money bar menu provides a chance to take on a full English breakfast, a light lunch, or something a bit more substantial like one of their succulent steaks. The restaurant offers a high-quality Continental-British menu, coupled with an impressive wine list, and diners can enjoy a panoramic view of the golf course and the nearby lakes, fountains, and water fowl. *Weald of Kent Golf Course, Maidstone Road, Headcorn, Kent TN27 9PT Tel: 01622 891671 / 890866 Fax: 01622 891793*

Pluckley *Map 2 ref H6*
18 miles SE of Maidstone on the B2077

This little village clusters around a tidy little square and the surrounding cottages all have a curious feature - *"Dering"* windows. These windows were added by a 19th century landowner, who considered the style lucky because one of his ancestors had escaped through one such window during the Civil War. He put them into his own mansion but with a singular lack of luck since the great house burnt down. The village claims to be very haunted, with as many as nine types of ghost having been reported.

The attractive hamlet of Munday Bois near Pluckley is the setting for **The Rose and Crown**, a traditional Kent pub with a devoted local following. The pub began as an ale house for local farm labour-

The Rose and Crown

ers in 1780, and it has been licensed ever since. Owners Michael and Joanna (Jo) Rainbird are popular hosts, and Jo is an accomplished Cordon Bleu chef who recently won a prize in the Steak and Kidney Pie Competition sponsored by the Meat and Livestock Commission. This goes well with her first prize in the 1996 Mobil Pub Meal of the Year competition. The interior is traditional but not in the least cramped while outside there is a large and pretty garden with a special children's play area. The Rose and Crown is popular with cyclists, some of whom are French, and Morris dancing in the summer adds to the prevailing atmosphere of Merry Old England. *The Rose and Crown, Munday Bois, Pluckley, Kent Tel: 01233 840393*

Charing   Map 2 ref H5
18 miles SE of Maidstone on the A20

Although there are a number of modern houses along the Ashford Road Charing preserves a much older core tucked behind the highway. Many of these houses date from the 15th and 16th centuries and many have overhanging storeys. There was once a palace belonging to the Archbishop of Canterbury here; after the Dissolution under Henry VIII, however, it fell into decay and its remains are now part of a farmhouse.

The tower of **Saints Peter and Paul** parish church is over 600 years old but the remainder was rebuilt at the end of the 16th century after a disastrous fire. There are lovely painted beams on its medieval roof and among its possessions is a vamp horn, one of very few in existence; these instruments were important elements in medieval church orchestras.

Through the Downs to the sea

Hollingbourne   Map 2 ref G5
5 miles E of Maidstone off the A20

With its adjoining hamlet, Eyhorne Street, Hollingbourne forms a linear village stretching out below the North Downs. Eyhorne Street is the older of the two sections and has a number of timber-framed and traditional weatherboard houses. A meadow, crossed by a railway line, separates it from Upper Hollingbourne which has fine views, particularly from the churchyard of **All Saints Church**. Near the church are the ruins of **Hollingbourne Manor**, which are said to be haunted by Catherine Howard, the fifth wife of Henry VIII. Easily seen from the road, the Manor is closed to the public.

A soothing atmosphere created by old oak beams and a large

The Windmill

inglenook fireplace is a clue to the popularity of **The Windmill**, which is only five minutes' drive from Leeds Castle in the village of Hollingbourne. The pub, which is off the Pilgrim's Way, almost certainly takes its name from a windmill that once stood nearby. Such an open location would have been ideal for a windmill; now it provides a lovely vantage point for extensive views from the large garden. The inglenook fireplace dominates the interior of the pub - in places by the side of the fire the stone is carved away where knives were once sharpened before carving meat. The pub was originally a coaching inn, and parts of the building have been dated back to 1460. Managers Mandy Lindley and Sean Staniforth can provide more information about the pub's history, sending visitors on hunts through the pub to detect evidence of its age. They also oversee the wide range of food on offer, and the calendar is punctuated with special meals enlivening Pancake Day, Valentine's Night, and other occasions. *The Windmill, Eyhorne Street, Hollingbourne, near Maidstone, Kent ME17 1TR   Tel: 01622 880280*

Harrietsham
Map 2 ref G5

7 miles E of Maidstone on the A2

With views stretching south towards the Weald of Kent and the wooded slopes of the North Downs at its back, Harrietsham has an enviable situation. In years gone by, however, a different aspect of its location was foremost in people's minds - it stands about a quarter of the way from Maidstone to Folkestone, with what is now the A2 having been the principal route to the Channel ports.

Some of the best views of the Weald of Kent can be savoured at **The Pepperbox Inn**, which is located on the evocatively named Windmill Hill by the village of Fairbourne Heath. This is a fine old-fashioned pub, with plants climbing the white exterior. Inside there is a wonderful old fireplace with inglenook seats; the main seating area also has sofas and armchairs to make patrons feel very much at home. Converted oil and gas lamps, and hops hanging from the low ceilings create a natural, genuinely rural feel. This homely, wel-

The Pepperbox Inn

coming atmosphere can only develop over time and visitors will not be surprised to learn that the Pepperbox Inn has been owned by the same family for 40 years. Geoff and Sarah Pemble make ideal hosts, every bit as natural with muddy ramblers as they are with passing business folk. The Pepperbox also provides patrons with a wide range of top-quality food, which can also be eaten on the large patio outside. Well lighted at night, the patio is the ideal vantage point for admiring the outstanding views. *The Pepperbox Inn, Windmill Hill, Fairbourne Heath, Harrietsham, Maidstone, Kent ME17 1LP Tel: 01622 842558*

The little hamlets surrounding Harrietsham are remarkably picturesque, with traditional architecture visible in the tile-hung cottages and even some vestiges of Medieval buildings.

Nestled off the beaten track in the North Downs, yet only five minutes' drive from both Leeds Castle and junction 8 of the M20, is **The Ringlestone Inn and Farmhouse Hotel**. This unspoilt medieval tavern, faced by a farmhouse hotel, offers diners and guests a chance to step back in time. The inscription, dating from 1632, on the English oak sideboard is as valid today as it was more than three and a half centuries ago: *"A Right Joyouse and welcome greetynge to ye all"*. The inn was built by monks as a hospice in 1533 and became an ale house around 1615. Much of the inn has changed very little since then, and the interior retains its original brick and flint walls and floors, inglenooks and furniture.

The Ringlestone Inn and Farmhouse Hotel

Traditional country recipes form the backbone of the hearty menu, and patrons are welcome to take their meal in either the candlelit dining room or by a roaring fire in one of the cosy bars. Outside are 8 acres of farmland and landscaped lawns, while facing the inn is the farmhouse, which provides accommodation of the highest order in rooms done out in rustic oak. *Ringlestone Inn and Farmhouse Hotel, Ringlestone Hamlet, Near Harrietsham, Maidstone, Kent ME17 1NX   Tel: 01622 859900*

Lenham   Map 2 ref H5
10 miles S of Maidstone on the A2

Another lovely village straddling the border between the North Downs and the Weald of Kent, Lenham has a timeless feel to it. A group of handsome buildings, some more than six centuries old, front the village square. The countryside to the north and south differs dramatically. To the north, hamlets such as **Warren Street** cling to the uplands of the North Downs. To the south it is a different matter: **Lenham Heath** is set in rolling, open countryside, a lovely village that preserves its distinctive identity despite lying just north of the M20.

Lenham provides the setting for **The Red Lion**, an attractive pub that dates back to the 14th century. Benches in the large open area to the front overlook the village square, offering the ideal perch for people-watching. To the rear is the courtyard - formerly the stables - where summer barbecues are popular. Bare brick walls, decorated with old pictures, surround the open-plan bar inside and there are three open fireplaces casting light playfully on the bare

The Red lion

wooden floors. Converted gaslamps and lamplights hang around the bar. The Red Lion offers a choice of five real ales - all cask - and there is home-made food available most lunchtimes and evenings. Fish, caught locally at Whitstable, is a speciality. *The Red Lion, The Square, Lenham, Maidstone, Kent ME17 2PG Tel: 01622 858531*

Sittingbourne
Map 2 ref H3

11 miles NE of Maidstone on the A2

The town of Sittingbourne calls to mind the days of heavily-laden barges making their way along the River Medway towards the mouth of the Thames. Many of these beautiful Thames barges were built at the boat yards around Sittingbourne. There were once as many as 11 boat yards here, but today only **Dolphin Yard** remains. Situated on the banks of Milton Creek near Crown Quay Lane, it is now a sailing boat museum. Although rather tucked away, this museum is really worth a visit to see the splendid barges with their ornate paintwork. Lovers of these romantic craft can trace their history and inspect several of them at close quarters.

To the north-west of Sittingbourne, you can pick up the A249 and head north to the twin archway of **Kingsferry Bridge**, which leads over the narrow tidal channel of the Swale to Sheppey.

Borden
Map 2 ref G3

10 miles NE of Maidstone off the A249

Backing on to Sittingbourne are a number of pretty villages. Borden, just a couple of miles south, lies in open countryside near the junction of the A249 and the M2. Like so many Kentish villages, it combines easy transport access with an unspoilt country atmosphere.

One of the most interesting attractions in the village of Borden, is **Oad Street Craft Centre**, a group of former farm buildings that have been imaginatively converted. Grouped around a central courtyard and surrounded by neat lawns, the buildings have maintained some of their traditional feel. The exposed beams blend well with the new brickwork and there is a sense of balance and space. The large showroom exhibits a wide range of unusual works including floristry, pottery, woodwork, jewellery, candles, metalwork, and glass.

Oad Street Craft Centre

In addition there is hot food and snacks served all day, ranging
from a refreshing cup of coffee to a three-course meal. *Oad Street
Craft Centre, Oad Street, Near Borden, Sittingbourne, Kent ME9
8LB   Tel: 01795 843130*

The Isle of Sheppey

Sheerness   Map 2 ref H2
17 miles E of Maidstone on the A249

Sheerness is the point at which the River Medway meets the Thames.
This was once the site of a naval dockyard, the first of them being
surveyed in the 17th century by none other than Samuel Pepys, the
famous diarist, who held the position of Secretary of the Admiralty
during the reign of Charles II. It was here, too, that HMS Victory
docked in 1805, bringing Nelson's body back home after the Battle
of Trafalgar. In recent years, Sheerness has developed into a busy
container and car-ferry port, and most of the island's prosperity is
centred here. Most of the town itself is made up of drab Victorian
housing for dockyard workers, and if it has a focal point at all it is
the rather odd blue clock tower in the High Street.

Minster   Map 2 ref I2
5 miles E of Sheerness off B2231

The unprepossessing seaside town of Minster is as unlikely a spot
as you could imagine to find one of the oldest sites of Christianity in
England. Nevertheless, it was here on the highest part of Sheppey
that Sexburga, the widow of a Saxon king of Kent, founded a nunnery in the latter part of the 7th century. Sacked by the Danes in
855 AD, **Minster Abbey** was rebuilt around 1130 and re-established
as a priory for Benedictine nuns; and in the 13th century, the parish
church was built adjoining the old monastic church or *"Nun's
Chapel"*. And so it was that from the Middle Ages until the time of
the Dissolution of the Monasteries, this ancient place served as a
"double church", the church of St Mary and St Sexburga, with the
nuns using the northern half of the building and the parishioners
worshipping in the southern section. These two distinct parts were
joined by an archway that was pierced in the south wall of the earlier Abbey church. To the west of the church is the 15th century
abbey gatehouse, which now houses a museum with exhibits on
Sheppey's history.

The sea has played an all-important role in the history of **La
Playa**, a lovely freehouse that stands on one of the best Blue Flag

La Playa

beaches in Kent. The building originally served as a yachting club; it gained its present name (meaning "beach" in Spanish) when it was converted to a pub in the 1980s. Licensees Edward and Elizabeth Moran were originally from Ireland, so there is no shortage of charm - or good conversation - in La Playa. Along with their two sons and two daughters they ensure that patrons are made welcome. Edward is a keen golfer and can offer advice and useful tips about the courses nearby. Outside the pub is a delightful garden with a fig tree, lanterns, and wooden seating. The sea also plays its part inside, and the view of the Channel from the large bar is memorable. There is a separate area for bar snacks as well as a large restaurant. Another attraction is afternoon tea, which patrons can have inside or out. La Playa is within easy walking distance of Minster Abbey; opposite, out at sea, lies the wreck of H.M.S. Montgomery, sunk in 1943. *La Playa, The Leas, Minster on Sea, Isle of Sheppey, Kent ME12 2NL   Tel: 01795 873059*

CHAPTER FIVE
Woodlands and Marshes

Romney Marsh

Chapter 5 - Area Covered

For precise location of places please refer to the colour maps found at the rear of the book.

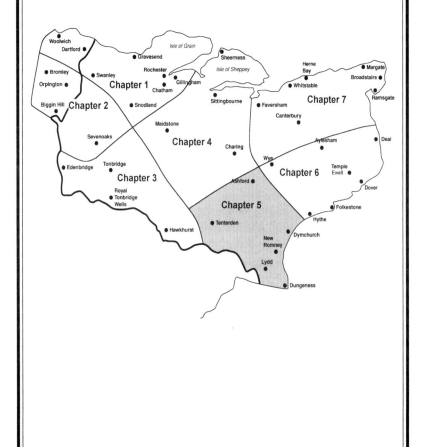

5
Woodlands and Marshes

Introduction

The region covered in this chapter comprises three of the most diverse - yet each in its own way defining - landscapes of Kent. Tenterden is the loveliest town in the Weald, although it really stands on the Weald's eastern fringe. Lovely villages lie to the west of Tenterden, their place-names often ending in *"-den"* to indicate their former settings as woodland clearings. Here, and to the south of Tenterden in the curiously named Isle of Oxney, are stretches of oak and beech woodlands that seem unchanged since medieval times or even earlier.

The Isle of Oxney really was an island, standing as a wooded hill in water before the surrounding Marsh gained a foothold where there was once the sea. It is this reclaimed land - naturally, here, unlike the hard-working efforts in Holland - that another defining Kentish landscape can be found. The Romney Marsh, along with the adjoining Walland and Denge marshes, is a place of eerie beauty, a remote setting of flooded meadows, drainage ditches and wind-bent trees that once was the haunt of smugglers. The changing nature of this landscape left some places *"high and dry"* - literally - when once they were thriving ports. Old Romney, Lydd and New Romney are interesting to visit today , but it is hard to imagine their past as thriving ports in the Middle Ages.

Lying to the east and north of these woodlands and marshes is that mainstay of the Kentish topography, rich farming country alongside rolling hills. Ashford, now an important European rail terminal, has played a traditional role in the trade from these Kentish farms and orchards.

Tenterden

Tenterden is known as the *"Jewel of the Weald"*, although it occupies a site that is right in the border between the dense woodlands of the Weald and the flatter, farming country that leads eastwards into the Romney Marshes. Today's well-earned nickname is a far cry from its earliest days, when it was known as *"Tenet-ware-den"*, or *"pig-pasture of the men of Thanet"*!

Despite the fact that pigs flourished here, sheep inevitably became the more profitable animal to farm on these fertile lands, and the wool trade quickly took off. In 1331, the far-sighted Edward III prohibited the export of unwashed wool and encouraged weavers

Tenterden High Street

from Flanders to settle here and bring their dyeing and weaving techniques to the English. The town of Tenterden and some of its neighbouring villages were to become the most important centres for the manufacture of broadcloth.

Once again, it was thanks to that earlier reclamation of the Romney Marsh that the area provided excellent grazing land, and brought about a profitable trade for the Wealden communities. Just outside Tenterden, Smallhythe and Reading Street provided access to the sea. These two small ports were founded as a means of transporting lumber from the Wealden forests, but by the 14th century, Smallhythe was firmly established as a boat-building centre.

The church of **St Mildred** can be found in the heart of Tenterden, and with its unusual twin doors at the western end, it is lovely. From the top of its 15th- entury tower - some 100 feet above the town - are far-reaching views across the Weald to the Channel Coast. Near the church is the **Town Hall** and the delightful Woolpack Inn, a proud reminder of the town's former days as a cloth trading centre. Another inn, the **William Caxton**, takes its name from the man who brought printing to England and who is said to have been born in Tenterden in 1422.

The centre of Tenterden stretches along its broad High Street, lined with shops and houses, nearly all with their original facades dating from the 16th to 18th centuries. Most of them, however, were built in a busy period between 1720 and 1760, so there is something of a Georgian feel to the town as a whole.

Located just of Tenterden High Street in an attractive little row of shops is **The Whistle Stop Cafe**, a popular tea room and ideal stop for a light meal. Proprietor Annie Oliver-Wanstall trained at catering college and has worked in a variety of hotels and pubs; she opened the Whistle Stop after taking a "career break" to have children. Annie's love of children is evident in the bright decor of this cosy tea room; knitted dolls festoon the room with its delightful lace-covered tables. She offers all manner of home-made cakes to accompany the hot drinks; cream teas are an afternoon favourite. In addition there is a chance to sample the all-day breakfast or - for a refreshing lunch - a choice of soups, salads, jacket potatoes and

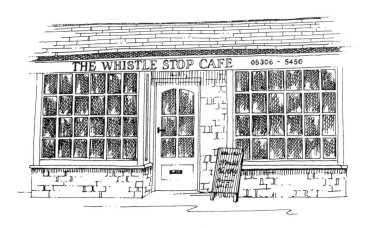

The Whistle Stop Cafe

sandwiches. Portions are generous and the service is friendly. A choice of gifts are displayed for sale around the shop. *The Whistle Stop Cafe, 2 Coombe Lane, Tenterden, Kent TN30 6HD Tel: 01580 765450*

Set back slightly from the traffic of the High Street but still very much in the heart of Tenterden is *Sparks Antiques Centre*, a collection of ten fascinating units trading in an astonishing range of antiques. Browsers and serious buyers rub shoulders among the displays of antique furniture, paintings, clocks, and collectibles. Overseeing this collections is proprietor Philip Ingham, whose knowledge and enthusiasm are infectious. The smaller units lead further and further back from the road until they reach *Sparks Antiques*, which can also be reached from the lane running alongside the premises.

Much larger than the units of Sparks Antiques Centre, this gives the items for sale a real stage on which to *"perform"*. A lovely chandelier hangs over the elegant furniture and objets d'art, which

Sparks Antique Centre

can be displayed in an uncluttered setting and viewed to full effect. The tired cliché about the past "coming alive" seems justified in this splendid setting, and rarely can antiques have been displayed in a more satisfying manner. *Sparks Antiques Centre and Sparks Antiques, 4 Manor Row, High Street, Tenterden, Kent TN30 6HP Tel: 01580 766696*

Sissinghurst to the Isle of Oxney

Sissinghurst   *Map 3 ref G7*
8 miles NW of Tenterden on the A262

The long village of Sissinghurst has many of the old-fashioned white-painted weatherboard houses, giving it a feel of architectural unity. Many of the larger houses were built by prosperous weavers, who worked in the thriving industry introduced during Edward III's reign. Nothing of this former industry remains, apart from these testaments to the wealth that the weaving created in the area.

Sissinghurst, of course, is famous for the lovely gardens which were the creation of the writer Vita Sackville-West and her husband Harold Nicolson. The couple bought *Sissinghurst Castle* in 1930 and their purchase was in reality a wreck. Previously, during the Seven Years War, it had housed up to 3,000 French prisoners and the only part of the castle left standing after its role as a prison ended - and decades of neglect added their toll - was a workhouse. The pair restored what they could of the house and set about creating gardens in its grounds.

Sissinghurst Castle

The garden is a wonder and a true testament to their creative spirit. Much of it is laid out in Elizabethan style; of particular interest is the White Garden planted entirely with silver-leafed white-flowering species, separated by box hedges. This garden, and the others, are set out as if they were *"rooms"*, each with a different theme. Spring and summer brings a delightful scent of herbs, which are another speciality of the garden.

Benenden
Map 3 ref G7

7 miles W of Tenterden on the B2086

Benenden stands in the dense Wealden woodlands that lie west of Tenterden. It is most famous for its girls' school, also called **Benenden**, which is housed in a mock-Elizabethan house built in 1859. The village itself is a quiet and tranquil settlement, with houses ranged round the large green, on which cricket is played on most summer evenings.

Rolvenden
Map 3 ref G8

3 miles SW of Tenterden on the A28

Rolvenden stands in wooded countryside just by the eastern fringe of the Weald known as the Isle of Oxney. It has a similar feel to Benenden but there is a greater sense of activity, partly because it lies along the road linking Tenterden with Hastings to the south. Along Rolvenden High Street is the **C.M. Booth Collection of Historic Vehicles**, which has a fascinating assortment of vintage cars, motorcycles and bicycles.

Small Hythe
Map 3 ref H8

5 miles S of Tenterden on the B2082

It is hard to imagine that this little hamlet on the road between Tenterden and Hythe was once a flourishing port and ship-building centre. Yet during the Middle Ages the river Rother flowed past wide and deep enough to accommodate ships of the period. One of Henry VIII's warships was built here. Today there is little trace of this industry or indeed of the river, which is only a tiny stream even in the wettest weather. One clue, however, lies in the name of the Small Hythe bus stop, which is called the Ferry, a reminder of past times.

Ellen Terry Museum, Smallhythe Place

The great actress Ellen Terry lived here and her home, Smallhythe Place, is now the **Ellen Terry Museum**. The museum offers a fascinating glimpse into her theatrical life but it would be worth visiting if only to examine the house, which was built in the late 15th century. It was originally the Port House and the home of a yeoman farmer. Much of the timber and the solid oak floors are original.

Wittersham   *Map 3 ref H8*
9 miles S of Tenterden on the B2082

Witttersham stands high in the middle of the Isle of Oxney, which was once a real island before the surrounding land was created from the sea itself. Its dominant setting has given it the affectionate title of the *"capital"* of the Isle, although it is hardly any larger or more important than the other attractive villages in the area. The only real evidence for its capital status is the spate of houses being built here, capitalising on the fine location. The skeleton of a prehistoric iguanadon was uncovered here and more recently it was a mooring site for airships during the First World War.

Situated in the village of Wittersham midway between the historic towns of Tenterden and Rye is **Lynford House**, a delightful and welcoming B & B which attracts guests who recognise its ideal location near the Channel Tunnel, the port of Dover, Sissinghurst, and the Dame Ellen Terry Museum. Owners Pam and Bill Hugget built this detached house in the traditional style in the early 1990's and are proud to invite guests to share in the pride they feel for this exceptional B & B. There are two rooms - a double and a twin - and both are spacious with colour-coded decor. Guests are encouraged

Lynford House

to explore the established gardens, with their roses, honeysuckle and even passion flower to give them an almost Mediterranean feel. There is secure parking and the pub opposite serves good food. *Lynford House, Swan Street, Wittersham, Kent TN30 7PH Tel: 01797 270182*

One of the most interesting buildings in Wittersham houses **Old Corner House Antiques and Picture Gallery**. It seems fitting that antiques should play such a large role in today's business, since the house itself has been the subject of intense historical scrutiny. For generations it was the only shop in Wittersham, known as Neve's Shop after the family whose ancestors arrived in the late 16th century when the Huguenots were expelled from France. There is evidence that the core of the house dates back to that period, and

Old Corner House Antiques and Picture Gallery

with the property remaining in the same family's hands for so long, it would seem churlish to dispute its pedigree. Today's owner, Fred Shepherd, can offer all manner of stories about the house, but the main attraction now is his well-displayed collection of antiques and pictures. Browsers and serious buyers are equally welcome, and there is useful advice about purchases, restoration, and transport. *Old Corner House Antiques and Picture Gallery, 6 Poplar Road, Wittersham, near Tenterden, Kent TN30 7PG Tel: 01797 270236*

On the western edge of the Isle of Oxney, at Moons Green on the outskirts of Wittersham, is **Oxney Farm**, a charming B&B set in peaceful rural surroundings in the countryside midway between Tenterden and Rye. Lying back from the lane, and surrounded by its own fields and neighbouring farms, it enjoys wide-ranging views

Oxney Farm

over the Rother Levels. Owner Eve Burnett extends a warm *"home from home"* welcome to guests who may arrive as strangers but leave as friends. Winner of the silver *"Welcome to Kent"* Hospitality Award 1996, Oxney Farm also comes with the Tourist Board's Two Crowns Highly Commended grading and is a non-smoking house. There are three spacious rooms for guests, and a seven-day rate provides exceptionally good value. Guests also have the use of the luxurious indoor swimming pool from April to September. The farm is run as the Isle of Oxney Miniature Equine Centre; the presence of these horses adds to the charm and friendly country house atmosphere. Eve and her husband Brian are happy to offer advice on the many places of historical, scenic, and cultural interest within easy reach. The farm has ample parking. Oxney Farm is easily reached; turn off the B2082 at the Swan Inn, Wittersham into Swan Street; Oxney Farm is 1.3 miles along on the left. *Oxney Farm, Moons Green, Wittersham, Kent TN30 7PS Tel: 01797 270558 Fax: 01797 270958*

Stone-in-Oxney   *Map 3 ref H8*
11 miles SE of Tenterden off the B2082
Stone-in-Oxney has a striking situation on the eastern flank of the inland island known as the Isle of Oxney. The **Stone** that gives the village its name is Roman in origin and is preserved in the parish church of St Mary's. There are other archaeological remains within the church indicating that it once served as a temple to Mithras, a Persian deity beloved of Roman soldiers. The church, like the village itself, looks eastwards across the damp marshes.

From Tenterden to Ashford

Biddenden *Map 3 ref G7*

6 miles N of Tenterden on the A262

Biddenden lies at the end of the A274 at the junction with the A262. Quite apart from the physical attractions of its architecture and picturesque High Street - crammed with pubs, restaurants and antique shops housed in fine half-timbered buildings - there is something else here that has assured the village of a permanent place in the history books. Way back around the beginning of the 12th century, two of its most famous residents were born. These were the *"Biddenden Maids"*, Eliza and Mary Chulkhurst, who were Siamese twins joined at the hips. Rare enough today, the presence of Siamese twins in a medieval community was an occurrence of unheralded novelty.

One of the finest of Biddenden's houses can be found just to the north of the village green. This is the **Old Cloth Hall**, a superb six-gabled building which was the centre of the local cloth trade in medieval and Tudor times, and housed the workshops of the weavers. As you enter the village, the road takes you past the beautifully maintained church. All Saints Church dates from Saxon times, the earliest parts remaining today are the nave, chancel and south aisle dating from the late 13th century.

High Halden *Map 3 ref H7*

4 miles N of Tenterden on the A28

High Halden stands in the delightful countryside lying east and north of Tenterden. Less wooded than the Weald, which begins just 5 miles to the west and can be seen clearly, and more undulating than the marshes to the south, the land here is rolling and given over to orchards and farms. It makes a wonderful spot to stop and admire the gentle transition of landscapes that characterises the land that is north of the Isle of Oxney and west of the Romney Marsh.

Set in the lovely countryside just a minute's drive north of High Halden village is **Ransley Oast**, which provides memorable self-catering accommodation in a converted oast house. The building, unchanged in its original oast house exterior, stands in a lovely setting with fields on all sides. Inside, however, guests can marvel at the imaginative conversion of this building from its original hop-drying function to its new role as an expansive self-catering suite. The main room is round, with exposed beams and a high pointed roof. Windows set at floor level create an unusual and pleasant ef-

fect. Given the prevalence of wood on all sides, it is not surprising that owner Emma MacLennan insists on a no-smoking policy. A separate fully equipped kitchen, large bathroom and spacious lounge are the other features in this one-of-a-kind apartment, which features panoramic views from all sides. There is good off-road parking, and pathways and walks lead in all directions from Ransley Oast.

Ransley Oast

Guests can explore the local woodlands or make their way to the Chequers pub for a good meal. *Ransley Oast, Ashford Road, High Halden, Ashford, Kent TN26 3LL*

Smarden
Map 3 ref G6

12 miles N of Tenterden on the B2077

Smarden's name comes from a Saxon word meaning *"butter valley and pasture"*. Despite the heavy traffic which it is forced to contend with, the main street is one of the finest in the county, with beautiful old houses on either side. At the western end stands a picturesque group of weatherboarded houses with tiled roofs, and the early-14th century church - known as the *"Barn of Kent"* due to its scissors-beam roof with intersecting timbers - stands surrounded by trees. Access to the churchyard is beneath a low arch formed by the overhanging first storey of a delightful timbered building called the *Penthouse*.

Located just a few minutes' drive from the charming village of Smarden is *Blinks Farmhouse*, where Sheila and Tony Brown ensure that B&B guests are made welcome and comfortable in their 16th century farmhouse. Sheila, a former actress and television interviewer, has found her real love - living in the country as a potter

Blinks Farmhouse

and painter. She is just as comfortable in her role as hostess: "I love cooking, and I love my house and garden. Nothing is nicer than when pleasant people visit us to share them." Lovingly restored, Blinks Farmhouse has a peaceful setting amid hop gardens. The three guest rooms are en suite and guests can unwind in the sitting room with its log fires, exposed oak timbers and television. The terrace outside overlooks the large garden and the enclosed heated swimming pool. *Blinks Farmhouse, Haffenden Quarter, Smarden, Ashford, Kent TN27 8QR Tel: 01233 770471*

Bethersden
Map 3 ref H7

9 miles NE of Tenterden on the A28

The name Bethersden is now associated with its "marble", which is actually a type of fossil-encrusted stone which appears in many Kent churches and in its two cathedrals. The village itself lies along the main Tenterden to Ashford road. Notwithstanding this crucial location - and in addition the abundance of local building materials in the form of its famous stone - Bethersden was reckoned to have had the worst roads in Kent in the 18th century.

Kent's reputation as the Garden of England is justified, and visitors to the Weald country should stop at **Stone Green Nurseries** if they detect a certain green tinge developing on their fingers. The nurseries cover nearly 2 hectares in verdant countryside; it is about 6 km from Tenterden along the Old Surrenden Manor Road towards Pluckley. The nurseries are open on selected weekends between April and September; the exact dates can be confirmed over the telephone. The nurseries were established in 1994 and have already become renowned for their extensive range of clematis, of which there are

Stone Green Nurseries

some 150 varieties on offer. These range from small alpine varieties to large flowering hybrids and include scented and non-scented varieties. Also on offer are hardy shrubs, more than 300 types of foliage plants, 30 varieties of grasses and cordylines (spiky plants). Owner Emma Knox can advise customers on their purchases and provides imaginative suggestions based on her range of climbing plants and patio plants. There is ample parking and good wheelchair access. *Stone Green Nurseries, Pluckley Road, Bethersden, Ashford, Kent TN26 3DD   Tel: 01233 820998*

Ashford   Map 3 ref I6
15 miles NW of Tenterden on the A28

Ashford still boasts some fine Georgian houses, and the earliest parts of the splendid parish church date back to the 15th century. The great central tower rises above the town, each of its four lofty pinnacles crowned by a golden weathervane shaped like an arrow. Ashford's central location makes it one of the most convenient touring centres in the county. It is a convenient spot altogether - you can get to Folkestone within 15 minutes with Hythe and New Romney just 20 minutes away. Leeds Castle is also near by, as are Chatham Historic Dockyards and Chilham Castle.

Ashford is proud of the fact that it had the first volunteer Fire Service in the country. It was formed in 1826, and in 1836 purchased its first manual fire engine. It was here in 1925 that the first Leyland motor fire engine was put into service, all funds having been raised by public subscription. The original fire station has now sadly gone, in its place stands the Boots store.

An original 1916 British Mark IV tank, one of only three in existence, can be found standing proudly in **St George's Square**. It was presented to the people of Ashford in recognition of their splendid response to the war efforts in World Wars I and II. The tank is now designated as a listed building!

The newly opened *Channel Tunnel Terminal* is already a huge influence on the town, as Ashford is the only passenger boarding point between London and the continent. 10 to 15 services per day link Ashford to Lille, Paris or Brussels. The journey from Ashford to Paris takes about two hours.

South to the Romney Marsh

Woodchurch
Map 3 ref H7

5 miles E of Tenterden off the B2067

Woodchurch is a large village set on a gentle slope. There are many lovely houses - one Tudor and a number from the Georgian period - facing its large green, which is in the heart of the village. It was on this green, in 1826, that a battle took place between a smuggling gang and the dragoons. The culprits were convicted and sentenced to transportation to Australia.

With an enviable south-facing location on the expansive village green of Woodchurch, *Prospect House* is well placed to offer B&B accommodation and dinners of the highest quality. The house itself, dating from 1789 and now a listed building, stands in its own gardens - the living room and the two guest bedrooms all overlook the

Prospect House

green and the woodlands that fringe this lovely village. Mrs Fiona
Adams-Cairns, the owner, provides a hospitable welcome that sets
one in mind of a house party. Guests soon fall into the comfortable
feeling that they are guests in a private house. Fiona has furnished
Prospect House with antiques. A no-smoking rule makes Prospect
House even more inviting, and guests have the chance to take their
evening meal here as well. *Prospect House, Woodchurch, Ashford,
Kent TN26 3PF Tel: 01233 860285*

Warehorne
Map 3 ref I8

9 miles E of Tenterden off the B2067

The village of Warehorne stands on a ridge overlooking Romney
Marsh. It is also a good place from which to explore this strange
landscape of broad dikes, stunted trees, drainage ditches and
swampy reedbeds. One of the best, and safest, ways of exploring is
to follow the course of the **Royal Military Canal** to Appledore. The
Canal, this stretch of which is owned by the National Trust, was
built in the first decade of the 19th century as a means of flooding
Romney Marsh in the event of an (expected) Napoleonic invasion.
The Martello towers along the coast, and strategically located gun
emplacements, were also part of this overall defensive strategy. Ironically, by the time the Canal was completed in 1807 the threat of
invasion had ended.

Snargate
Map 3 ref I8

10 miles SE of Tenterden on the B2080

Snargate lies in the heart of the Romney Marsh and its remote location conjures up the days when smugglers plied their illicit trade in
the cover of darkness, hiding their booty along reed-lined streams
or in some of the disused, almost inaccessible farm buildings. The
parish church is in an exposed position and the first impression
many people have of this 600 year-old building is that it seems dis-
proportionately large for such a small village. This extra capacity
was a boon for smugglers in bygone days and the church was used
as a storage room. An excise raid in 1743 uncovered a cask of gin in
the vestry and tobacco in the belfry.

Brookland
Map 3 ref I8

12 miles SE of Tenterden on the A259

Brookland has a marshland setting that lives up to its name. Here,
where the southern fringes of Romney Marsh give way to the even
more remote Walland Marsh, is a landscape of flooded meadows,
small ditches and dikes. Brookland possesses an unusual architec-

tural feature in the form of the **belfry** of its parish church, St Augustine's. The belfry, built in three vertical wooden stages, stands quite apart from the rest of the church, in much the same way that the campanile of an Italian church or cathedral is separate. The belfry dates from the 13th century and architectural historians surmise that the builders feared that the church, built on such damp foundations, would not support the extra weight of the belfry. Inside the church are a number of interesting features, the most notable of which is the Norman font containing scenes of daily life - providing a wonderful *"slice of life"* snapshot of the Middle Ages.

Old Romney   *Map 3 ref I8*
13 miles SE of Tenterden on the A259

Old Romney, with its setting in the remote Romney Marsh which takes its name, has a forlorn feel that somehow calls to mind the tale of Ozymandias. It seems improbable, looking at today's quiet village with its small church, scattered cottages, and pub, that it was once a productive port. The Domesday Book records three fisheries, a mill and a wharf, indicating its waterfront setting. As the marsh gained more land from the

Romney Marsh

sea, Romney's position - which had been as a busy island - became landlocked and trade became hampered considerably. It lost out to New Romney, which ironically also found itself a victim of the gradually accretion of land in the Marsh.

Lydd   *Map 3 ref I9*
16 miles SE of Tenterden on the B2076

Like Old Romney, Lydd was once a busy port, linked to the Cinque port of New Romney. The changing course of the River Rother, coupled with the steady build-up of land along the Marsh, meant that

Lydd was no longer a port by the late Middle Ages. It now lies nearly three miles from the sea, bereft of its original reason for growth, but still containing some mementoes of its prosperous past. The centre of Lydd has some fine merchants' houses as well as a handsome **guildhall** and its parish church, **All Saints**, has been described as the *"Cathedral of the Marshes"*. The church took a direct hit from a German bomb in the Second World War but was painstakingly restored. About two miles south of Lydd, near Boulderswall Farm, is **Dungeness Bird Reserve**, which is an informative ornithological centre managed in part by the RSPB.

Dungeness   *Map 3 ref J10*
20 miles SE of Tenterden off the B2076

Dungeness has a perverse attraction for many people. It lacks any charm and warmth, apart from the discharge from its nuclear power station, and yet visitors to the Romney Marsh feel compelled to go that bit further to reach this southeastern corner of Kent. There is a motley collection of jerry-built fishermen's shacks and a makeshift boardwalk enables people to negotiate the loose shingle of this stretch of coast. Notwithstanding the power station, the modern lighthouse and the curious hubbub of fishermen, Dungeness offers the chance to contemplate the military battles of the Spanish Armada, the former smuggling trade and the importance generally of the Channel to England's character.

New Romney   *Map 3 ref I8*
16 miles SE of Tenterden on the A259

The peaceful little town of New Romney is known as the *"capital"* of the Marsh, one of the five original Cinque Ports, and headquarters of the **Romney, Hythe & Dymchurch Railway**. The station - roughly midway between the town and the seafront - contains workshops and the various engines in their sheds. Those keen on even smaller-scale models will also find the **Romney Toy & Model Museum** here. Vintage models, toys and photographs are on display, and there are two working model railways to enjoy.

A great storm in 1287 diverted the course of the River Rother and choked it with shingle, causing it to flow into the sea at Rye and leaving the port of Romney without a harbour. To see just how high the flood waters rose, you have only to visit the splendid Norman **church of St Nicholas**, where the floodmarks can be seen high up on the pillars inside. This disaster was a severe blow to the town's former days of glory as one of the most important of the Cinque Ports.

Dymchurch

Map 3 ref J8

21 miles E of Tenterden on the A259

From Hythe heading along the A259 you can make your way down the coast towards Dymchurch. At various points along the road, you will notice those decidedly odd and not especially attractive buildings, the **Martello Towers**. Looking more like the truncated cooling towers of a modern power station than the pride of Britain's defence against Napoleon, there were at one time 74 of these massive "pepper pots" positioned along the coast. Their name derives from the fact that they were constructed along the lines of a tower at Cape Mortella in Corsica; an ironic choice of model bearing in mind that Napoleon himself was born on that particular island!

At one time a quiet, secluded village, Dymchurch has now been transformed into a busy seaside resort. Amusement arcades, giftshops and cafes line the road, and you need to park the car and clamber over the formidable **Dymchurch Wall** before you can even catch a glimpse of the reason why everybody comes here! The sea-wall is the only thing that prevents the sea from flooding both town and marsh - Dymchurch lies about seven and a half feet below high-tide level - and a barrier of one sort or another has existed here since the Romans came to Kent.

Occupying a position at the top of the high street in Dymchurch is **Ann's Crafts and Haberdashery**, owned by Ann Dennis who has lived in the area for 35 years and has run this shop for 25 years, having changed it from a hairdressers in 1994. Her experience of craft is important, because Ann has built up a number of contacts with local craftspeople in the Romney Marsh area. Her shop specialises in unique gift items, all hand-made by local people, a testimony to the inventive traditions of the area. Customers *"pop in"* for a moment and then find themselves in a marvellous world of wax or

Ann's Crafts and Haberdashery

cross-stitch pictures, decoupage, embroidery, birthday cards and a host of kits and ornaments. As well as haberdashery and craft supplies, a range of porcelain dolls from three major manufacturers is stocked, and there is a large range of Craftime vinyl dolls and dress patterns for customers who wish to create their own little friends. *Ann's Crafts and Haberdashery, 13 High Street, Dymchurch, Romney Marsh, Kent TN29 0NH   Tel: 01303 872177*

Burmarsh
Map 3 ref J8

24 miles E of Tenterden off the A259

Burmarsh lies at the northern end of the Romney Marsh, and for holidaymakers from the Channel Ports it provides the first glimpse of this remote corner of Kent. A narrow ditch crosses the sometimes flooded marshland meadows and leads to the parish church and the local inn, the Shepherd and Crook. It is in this sort of old-fashioned inn that patrons expect to hear tales of rum-runners, wreckers, owlers or marsh pilots - all of which were terms used to describe local smugglers.

Donkey Street, which twists its way either from Dymchurch and Burmarsh or from West Hythe and Botolph Bridge, leads past **Lathe Barn**, a rural hideaway featuring farmhouse teas, a farm museum, a children's farm, and a gift shop. When Janet and Richard Andrew converted an old farm building into a house and tea room in 1979, some sceptics said that their out of the way location took *"off the*

Lathe Barn

beaten track" just one stage too far. Of course, this seeming remoteness only adds to the charm, and the farm itself stands in 8 hectares (20 acres) of grassland.

The Tea Room offers old-fashioned light lunches, mouth-watering scones and cakes and a host of sundaes and ice-cream desserts.

The Museum offers a chance to explore the agricultural history of the area with its collection of farming and domestic items, ranging from Roman artefacts to Edwardian tools, with the largest implements in display outside. The grassland is home to Fred the donkey and his companions who include ponies, miniature pot-bellied pigs, geese, goats, rabbits, chickens, a peacock, calves, and owls. There is a play area for children and a putting green. *Lathe Barn, Donkey Street, Burmarsh, Romney Marsh, Kent TN29 0JN Tel: 01303 873618*

Lympne
Map 3 ref J7

21 miles E of Tenterden on the B2067

Pronounced *"Limm"*, Lympne is a former Roman port which was called Portus Lemanis. The Romans built a fort here in the 3rd century. It has been the victim of erosion and neglect but the remains, now known as **Studfall Castle**, can be visited. Only about 300 yards from there is **Lympne Castle**, a fortified manor house originally built in the 14th century. It was largely rebuilt early in this century but retains its original character. From the castle are far-reaching views over the Romney marsh, the Royal Military Canal and the Channel.

A pub has stood on the grounds of **The County Members** in Lympne since 1529, but the present pub was registered in 1852. The unusual name of the pub, however, is a throwback to the earlier date and refers to the seven MPs from Hythe who were major landowners in Lymph from the reign of Henry VIII to that of Victoria. The pub stands in rambling fields which stretch down to the marshes which are so prevalent in this part of Kent. Such a rural setting attracts nature lovers, ramblers from the Saxon Way and more than

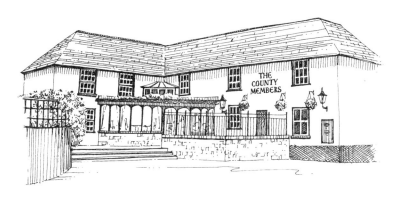

The County Members

a sprinkling of French and Dutch visitors eager for a first taste of English beer. The Makepeace family, who between them perform all the jobs, are friendly Yorkshire people who have settled easily into this quintessentially Kent inn. Special *"guest ales"* complement the range of Whitbread ales behind the bar. Also on offer is a food menu that caters to all tastes and appetites. There is also an imaginative choice of vegetarian dishes among the hearty meals available. *The County Members, Aldington Road, Lympne, Hythe, Kent CT21 4LH Tel: 01303 267748*

Hythe   *Map 4 ref K7*
22 miles E of Tenterden on the A259

The recorded history of Hythe goes back to 732 AD, when Ethelred, king of the Saxons, first granted it a charter. Its name means *"landing place"*, and the town once played an important role as one of the five Cinque Ports. Its decline in this respect came with the silting up of its harbour, which left it completely high and dry - it is now over half a mile from the sea and no trace of the harbour remains.

A mile to the north of Hythe is **Saltwood Castle**, which although not open to the public can be seen from a nearby bridleway. It was once the residence of the Archbishop of Canterbury, and it was here that Becket's murderers stayed the night on their way from France to do the evil deed. More recently it was the home of the late Lord Clark, the famous art historian and presenter of the pioneering television series, *"Civilisation"*. His son, Alan Clark MP, still lives here today.

CHAPTER SIX
Guarding the Channel

The Barbican, Sandwich

Chapter 6 - Area Covered

For precise location of places please refer to the colour maps found at the rear of the book.

6
Guarding the Channel

Introduction

Britain puts its best foot forward in the region surrounding Dover, as it stands within sight of France and is the acknowledged threshold to the Continent. The construction of the Channel Tunnel has not diminished the importance of Dover and Folkestone among Britain's ports of entry; each of them still thrives as nautical centres *par excellence*. If the Tunnel has done anything, however, it is to have spared some of the countryside around these two great ports; trains are already underground by the time they reach near-coastal villages which once felt the full force of Europe-bound traffic.

Eastern Kent is well aware of its role as the first port of call for visitors and invaders alike. Roman ruins and remnants abound, testimony of the vital role this region played in the defence of their northernmost imperial settlements. More recently, the hinterland behind Dover provided drill grounds for troops preparing to take on the might of Napoleon's army, and later still the whole coastline was a vital defensive network of gun emplacements, airfields and tunnel complexes poised to take on the threat of Hitler.

Yet despite the seemingly constant *"red alert"* nature of this area of Kent, there is a timeless, unfazed atmosphere running through its heart. It is here that bat trap and other traditional pub games seem to be most popular, undiluted by exposure to commercialsim and international traffic. Mills still stand, Art Deco hotels recall the days of flappers and hip flasks, but most of all the area around this coast seems to epitomise the quintessentially English elements so dear to former Prime Minister John Major. Here, within sight of the Continent, you can expect to find spinsters riding their bicycles to Evensong, cricketers playing in the waning light, and hearty villagers downing bitter in their local pub.

Dover

The ancient town of Dover is Britain's major cross-Channel port. Known as the *"Gateway to England"* to those coming in, it is also one of the major routes to Europe for those going out. From here you can take a jetfoil, hovercraft or ferry to Calais, Boulogne, Zeebrugge or Ostend, and your choice of transport will soon be extended to include the new giant catamarans - although for our part, we were more than happy to stay in Dover a while!

Dating back to 1180, the massive **Dover Castle** sits astride a high hill above the clifftops, dominating the town from almost every angle. It was here on the site of an Iron Age fort that the Normans built this impressive stronghold during the last years of Henry II's reign at the then colossal cost of nearly £7,000, and today it ranks among the greatest fortresses in Western Europe.

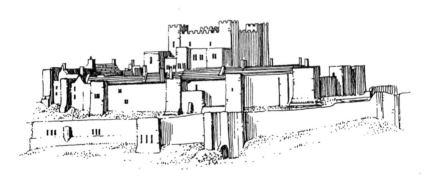

Dover Castle

Apart from an impressive 19th century scale model of the Battle of Waterloo which is displayed in one of the first floor rooms, the chambers and passageways are relatively bare - yet the Castle exerts a forceful presence and it is not hard to visualise it as a busy working garrison, teeming with life.

Of course, Dover has many other attractions besides its castle. One of the most popular of these, **The Roman Painted House**, can be found in New Street in the centre of the town. The main features of this Roman town house are a complex system of underfloor heating and the most beautifully preserved painted walls. First discovered in 1970, the house has won various awards for the way in which it has been preserved, and excavation is currently still in progress. One of the team, Wendy Williams, has put together a very special display using the features of those who once lived here. Working on the skulls excavated at the site, she has painstakingly built up their features to produce an uncanny group of extremely lifelike faces.

At first sight, the Victorian Town Hall in the High Street may not look as though it warrants any special attention, but if you step inside you will find that it incorporates the magnificent **Maison Dieu**, a hostel for Canterbury pilgrims which was originally founded in 1203. Beneath the building lie the cells of **Dover Old Town Gaol**, now open to the public throughout the year. Starting in the Court Room, your tour will take you back in time to the horrors of prison life during the Victorian era, including a visit to the exercise yard, washroom and cells. The prisoners and gaolers themselves relate their stories to you, courtesy of 'hi-tech' talking heads and the very latest animation and audio-visual techniques.

While you are in the town centre, you can hardly fail to notice the modern glass and chrome building facing the Market Square, which houses Dover's exciting visitor attraction. It is called **The White Cliffs Experience**. Here you will find yourself being drawn into *"live"* action. You can chat to a centurion, encounter the warring Cantiacii tribe who greeted the Roman invaders, experience life as a galley slave, and wander through the rubble of a typical Dover street after it has endured the horrors of a World War II air raid attack.

All this and more takes place in the *'Historium'*, and in addition there is a Museum with three floors full of displays on the history of Dover from its earliest beginnings to the present day; the Archaeological 'Gardens' featuring the remains of the Norman church of St Martin-le-Grand and those of the *'Classis Brittanica'*, the headquarters of the Roman fleet in England; together with a cinema, a themed restaurant and coffee shop, a top-floor research centre which is open to visitors, an educational resource centre and a gift shop. All in all, this is a stimulating and unforgettable experience which all members of the family will enjoy - and you will need to set aside several hours of the day to fully appreciate all that the attraction has to offer.

Crabble Corn Mill

Standing alongside the River Dour in Dover is **Crabble Corn Mill**, which is the largest working watermill in the South East. Crabble Mill was built in 1812 to fed the thousands of troops who were defending Dover against the threat of invasion by Napoleon. It continued to operate for 81 years until its water-powered machinery lost out to the advent of electrical power in the 1890's. After languishing closed for 70 years Crabble Mill was restored and reopened. Visitors can now take a Mill tour, grinding corn by the excellent displays and feeling the samples at each stage of making flour. The Mill Gallery plays host to regularly changing exhibitions of local craftspeople and artists and the gift shop sells local crafts as well as Crabble flour for home baking. The cafe serves lunch, teas, and snacks featuring the best of Kentish ingredients. *Crabble Corn Mill Trust, Lower Road, River, Dover, Kent CT17 0UY Tel: 01304 823292/824930*

Pickwicks, a popular pub in the attractive area around Dover known as the River, has had its current name since 1983. The Dickensian flavour of the new name reflects the era in which it was built. In 1863, land from Kearnsey Manor Farm was set aside to build a new inn, the Railway Bell Hotel, and - true to its name - a bell outside the pub was rung for ten minutes before the approach of a train. These days the call to "drink up please" is more likely to

Pickwicks

come from proprietor Bob Allen, whose local popularity has helped maintain the pub's draw on local residents. The train link was far from lost with the name change: a fascinating collection of railway paraphernalia, pictures, and artefacts from the steam age adorn the walls. A large open plan bar is surrounded by the public area, which includes seating for meals. The menu at Pickwicks ranges from quick and easy snacks to an assortment of tempting three-course meals, with an impressive wine list as well. The pub makes a good stop along local walks, which can take in the working 1812 water mill and the ruined abbey. *Pickwicks, 120 London Road, Kearnsey, Dover, Kent CT16 3AD   Tel: 01304 822016*

Around Dover

Folkestone   *Map 4 ref L7*
7 miles W of Dover on the A20
Folkestone is the second busiest cross-Channel port on the south coast. What is most unusual about this particular seaside resort is that it does not have a recognisable seafront as such; instead, it has **The Leas**, a series of delightful clifftop lawns and flower gardens with a distinctly Mediterranean feel to them, which run for a mile and a half from the centre of town towards Sandgate to the west. A water-driven lift takes residents from the clifftop hotels to the beach below, and the warm south-facing aspect makes this a very pleasant area to explore.

Much of Folkestone's history is conveniently condensed into an area known as *'The Lanterns'* on the Sandgate Road. The attractions centred in this part of town are many and varied. *The Bayle* was once the site of an ancient fort, and the lovely 13th century *Church of St Mary and St Eanswythe* (the oldest building in Folkestone) stands nearby. The bones of the latter patron saint are buried here.

Church Street, formerly called Mercery Lane, was home to the traders of silk and cloth, and William Harvey, one of England's most famous physicians, was born here in 1578. Perhaps Harvey's greatest gift to medicine was his discovery of the circulation of the blood; his statue can be seen near the centre of The Leas, appropriately clutching a human heart in his hand. It would seem, however, that all of Harvey's skills in the world of medicine came to naught when it came to his own fate, for he is reputed to have committed suicide in 1657 after discovering that he was going blind.

West Cliffe   Map 4 ref M6
3 miles NE of Dover off the A258

West Cliffe is a lovely small village set on the steep landscape of the South Foreland just north of Dover and near the much large St Margaret's at Cliffe. Wooded paths lead along the edge of the cliffs here, traversing the undulating land which at times resembles heaths, with rabbits running riot in places. West Cliffe makes an ideal vantage place for views over the Channel, and in particular looking south towards Dover and the site of the roman Pharos.

The first sighting of impressive *Wallett's Court* usually sets visitors' minds thinking of history, and the Oakley family, who run this imposing hotel, are only too happy to prove that the first impression is indeed correct. The present building, set in an open garden that merges into rolling fields, was built in the Elizabethan period but an earlier incarnation of Wallett's Court - known as the Manor of Westcliff - is mentioned in the Domesday Book. It became the property of Queen Eleanor of Castille, the wife of Edward I, in the 13th century and was for many years known as Queen Eleanor's Palace.

The Wallett's Court of today has absorbed the rich historical traditions and married them with a full range of modern comforts so that oak beams and Adam fireplaces are counterpointed by the colour television, en suite bathrooms, hairdryers, and all the accoutrements of pampered accommodation. Home-cooked food appears in the constantly changing table d-hote evening menu as well as the hearty breakfasts made with local farm produce. The nearness to Dover is a plus, and most visitors leave with wonderful

Wallett's Court

memories of their last - or first - night in England. *Wallett's Court, West Cliffe, St Margaret's Bay, Dover, Kent CT15 6EW   Tel: 01304 852424*

St Margaret's at Cliffe   *Map 4 ref M6*
6 miles NE of Dover on the B2058

St Margaret's at Cliffe has a location that is hard to surpass as a base for exploring the region around Dover. It stands a little way inland from St Margaret's Bay, which was a busy seaside resort before the Second World War, and which counted Noel Coward and Ian Fleming among its residents. The village itself has a setting high above the sea, and it was used as a gun emplacement to guard the Channel and protect against German invasion during the Second World War. Its 12th century parish church of **St Margaret of Antioch** has interesting rounded arches and an intricately carved doorway.

Ramblers are among the repeat customers at **The Hope Inn**, where they know they will find well-kept real ales and an appetite-battling menu at lunchtime and in the evening. Not everyone arrives on foot, and locals and tourists benefit from the spacious car park. The pub, which was built in 1736, is near the sea and is the nearest pub to St Margaret's holiday resort. Pleasant sea breezes drift across the sunny garden, which offers barbecues in the summer. Inside there is a large open-plan bar with a separate dining area as well as

The Hope Inn

a designated non-smoking area. Open fires blaze in the winter. Vic Lees, the licensee, has been in the trade for four decades and knows what sort of comforts and treats make customers happy - and likely to return. The sporting have a choice of skittles, darts, or pool but Vic knows that others might want, for example, a vegetarian meal, a play area for the children, or simply a cup of tea or coffee. It is this wide-ranging welcome that makes the Hope Inn special, and why its special events such as Valentines Day and Mothers Day, are so popular with locals and visitors alike. *The Hope Inn, High Street, Saint Margarets at Cliffe, near Dover, Kent CT15 6AT Tel: 01304 852444*

West through the Lyminge Forest

Denton Map 4 ref K6
10 miles NW of Dover off the A260

Denton is a charming village with a green surrounded by pretty half-timbered cottages. The handsome 18th century **Denton Court** can be found next to the church. Set in some 200 acres, this Victorian mansion was frequently stayed in by the poet Thomas Gray, of *"Elegy"* fame.

Exploring the country roads to the west of the A2 near here is another delight, and the charming cottages surrounded by pleasant green hedgerows and trees are a tonic to the city dweller.

Set back off the A260 in the tiny hamlet of Denton, roughly midway between Canterbury and Folkestone, is **The Jackdaw**, a traveller's inn that has been serving thirsty customers since the 17th century. In keeping with its origins as a coaching inn, the Jackdaw has a large car park, which is next to a spacious paved seating area to the front of the pub and facing some charming cottages. To the rear is an extensive garden, set away from the road and therefore safe for children. The interior is open plan, with old pictures, hops, flowers and brasses decorating the walls. Open fires create a cosy atmosphere and there are nook-like areas spread over different lev-

The Jackdaw

els where people can chat in small groups. The Jackdaw offers a range of foods, from light snacks to three or four-course meals, accompanied by a choice of fine wines. Managers Gary Knight and Clare Brewer ensure that the bar has a good selection of real ales. Film buffs might remember the Jackdaw as having featured in The Battle of Britain; wartime history and historical commemorations such as Bastille Day attract extra customers, especially from France. *The Jackdaw, The Street, Denton, near Canterbury, Kent CT4 6QY Tel: 01303 844663*

Barham   *Map 4 ref K5*
10 miles NW of Dover on the A2
Barham is set in a delightful river valley near the point where the woodlands of the North Downs give way to the flatter agricultural land that leads northwards towards the Isle of Thanet. Barham downs are mentioned in Arthurian legends as the site of a great battle and they were used as a military camp during the time when Britain expected a Napoleonic invasion.

The Elham Valley, with its lovely streams and pastures, provides an attractive setting for the **Elham Valley Vineyard**, which annually produces about 2,500 bottles of high-quality English wine from just over one hectare of vines. The vineyard represents an ambitious - and successful - plan by the Vale of Elham Trust to provide work and recreational opportunities for adults with learning difficulties. The work, with its added bonus of having a commercial purpose, is

Elham Valley Vineyard

an ideal way of building and maintaining self-esteem: workers are responsible for stock control, keeping the shop stocked with wine and for assisting in showing visitors around the winery. The Elham Valley Vineyard is planning to build - literally - on this success, and is aiming to upgrade facilities (including a shop and tearoom) and to provide for more daily worker placements. *Elham Valley Vineyard, Breach, Barham, Canterbury, Kent CT4 6LN Tel: 01227 831266*

Elham   *Map 4 ref K6*
15 miles W of Dover on the B2065
Yet another of the many Kent villages with a peculiarly pronounced place-name Elham (*"Eelham"*) is set in an attractive valley. The village is pleasant and relatively unspoilt despite a constant flow of tourist traffic in the area during summer months. It is the starting point for a number of footpaths leading through the Elham Valley, which is formed by the Nail Bourne stream running through lovely

meadows. Elham stands on a disused railway line which during the Second World War ran an 18-inch *"Boche Buster"* gun - actually of First world War vintage - which fired shells that were 7 feet long.

The delightful countryside in the heart of the Elham Valley - an designated Area of Outstanding Natural Beauty - provides a lovely setting for ***Parsonage Farm***. This family-run working farm stands on a site that has had a settlement for at least a millennium, and possibly much longer. The Palmer family have lived at Parsonage Farm for the last century of its extensive history, which features a long association with the University of Oxford since Edward I endowed Parsonage Farm to Merton College in 1267. On the wall is a copy - and translation - of this document. Visitors to the farm can follow trails around the farm, tracing six centuries of agricultural history. There are old and rare breeds of traditional farm animals,

Parsonage Farm

including sheep, cattle, pigs, horses, goats, chickens, and even a goose who thinks she is a chicken. Inside the distinctive Farmhouse is a fascinating small museum, with Grandfather George Palmer's old office in the Medieval undercroft. More history is on display in the Black Granary, Sutton's Granary, and in the outbuildings. The Shepherd's Hut offers home-cooked food all day and the shop sells preserves and souvenirs of the farm. An admission ticket to the farm is not needed here. *Parsonage Farm, North Elham, Canterbury, Kent Tel: 01303 840356/840766*

Stelling Minnis
Map 4 ref J6

17 miles W of Dover on the B2068

Stelling Minnis lies in the **Lyminge Forest** and on the main road - actually a pleasant B road - connecting Canterbury with Hythe. Luckily the forest has won the battle between nature and development and the village has an attractive rural atmosphere. Minnis meant *"common"* and today's open spaces reflect a sense of preservation which the Victorians applied - unlike other churches, the parish church here was not overly restored. There is also a lovely windmill on the outskirts of the village, from which one can enjoy views over the countryside leading southwards towards the village of Elmsted.

Elmstead
Map 4 ref J6

17 miles W of Dover off the 2068

Perched atop one of the highest points for miles around is **The Cottage With The View**, a charming B&B establishment that makes full use of its enviable location. The building itself, known as High Lodge, is a modernised and comfortable 250 year-old Kent farmhouse, which is just outside the centre of Elmsted and which lives up to its other name with its sweeping views over the Kent

The Cottage With The View

Downlands. A range of accommodation includes family, double and single bedrooms, and guests have the use of a sitting-room with books and television. A no-smoking establishment, The Cottage With The View is an excellent choice for families or indeed anyone who enjoys large gardens, panoramic views and a warm, unstuffy welcome. There are even pony rides for children. Mrs Jennifer Denny, the owner, can also provide evening meals, pack lunches and a wealth of information about the surrounding area. *The Cottage With The View, High Lodge, Elmsted, Ashford, Kent TN25 5JL Tel/fax: 01233 750234*

Brabourne
Map 4 ref J6
17 miles W of Dover off the B2068

Brabourne has a lovely setting just below the edge of the North Downs. An ancient inn stands at one end of the main street of this pretty village and locals must make their way along this street to the church. It is in the vicinity of the church that some of the prettiest houses stand, built by prosperous farmers for the most part and blending harmoniously with the flint-walled architecture of the church. Inside the church it is worth noting the window with its original 12th century glass.

Smeeth
Map 3 ref J7
14 miles W of Dover on the A20

Smeeth means *"a smooth clearing in the woods"*. Today most of the woods are gone, glimpsed just to the north, however, past the lovely village of Brabourne Lees and into the north Downs. Smeeth has a strong sense of identity, which can be glimpsed watching patrons playing traditional Kentish games at the local pub or in the way that the village has not lost the battle to the A20/M20 corridor, which runs nearby along the valley formed by the East Stour River.

The Woolpack is a welcoming local pub in the village of Smeeth near Ashford. Tenants Rod and Judy Vidler have run the Woolpack since May 1997 but they have lived in Smeeth for more than 20

The Woolpack

years and they are a popular pair. This is the sort of pub that forms the heart of a small community, and on a given evening - or lunchtime - new customers might find themselves rubbing shoulders with darts players, members of the quiz team, or the village cricketers slaking their thirst. There is even a chance to try bat and trap, a local Kentish game. Oak panelling throughout gives a warm feeling to the interior, helped by a double-sided open fire. Outside is a large garden with many attractions for children and a special barbecue patio for summer meals. A selection of hearty pub food is matched by a choice of real and cask ales. *The Woolpack, Church Road, Smeeth, near Ashford, Kent TN25 6RX Tel: 01303 812196*

Willesborough
Map 3 ref I6

17 miles W of Dover on the A20

Willesborough stands amid orchard country that owes more in its way to neighbouring Ashford than to Dover, some way to the east. The easy access to the M20, however, marks Willesborough as a good base from which to explore the western fringes of the Lyminge forest, which lies just to the north, past the village of Wye.

Although within easy reach of Junction 10 of the M20, *The Blacksmiths Arms* in Willesborough has all the attractions of an English village pub. Customers enter a timeless world of old brasses, wooden table and stools and blazing fires in inglenook fireplaces. Everything about the Blacksmiths Arms is traditional, from the low ceilings and leaded windows to the bare brick walls, hung with old plates and china. The pub features a good range of real ales and serves

The Blacksmith's Arms

hearty pub food. Managers Ted and Jan Kingston-Miles spent 17 years at the Black Horse in Pluckley (of *"Darling Buds of May"* fame) and they regale customers with amusing stories of times spent with the cast of the television series. The Blacksmiths Arms attracts an interesting mixture of customers, with holidaymakers and business people rubbing elbows with a loyal local following in the open plan bar area. Children are made especially welcome. Terraced lawns, with more than 30 picnic tables stretch out over the extensive garden and there is even a *"secret garden"* for children. *The Blacksmiths Arms, 84 The Street, Willesborough, Ashford, Kent TN24 0NA Tel: 01233 623975*

Wye
Map 3 ref I6

21 miles NW of Dover off the A28

Wye is an attractive market town which is steeped in history and is a delightful place to stay for a while, absorbing everything around you and perhaps taking time to visit the Romney, Hythe and Dymchurch Railway and the Romney Marshes, Dover Castle or historic Rye, all of which are no great distance away. Wye is also the home of the famous **Agricultural College**, which is affiliated to the University of London. The beautiful College buildings were built by John Kempe, who was born in the town in 1380 and went on to become Archbishop of Canterbury.

You will find that Wye is right in the heart of Kent, just 60 miles from London, with Ashford four miles away and the splendid cathedral city of Canterbury 12 miles away. Access to the M2 and M20 is simple, and Wye has a railway station with a direct service to London.

Boughton Aluph and Boughton Lees
Map 3 ref I6

22 miles W of Dover on the A251

The delightful villages of Boughton Aluph and Boughton Lees lie on the southern fringes of the North Downs, where wooded hills give way to a medley of hedgerows, meadows and fields, all traversed by narrow twisting lanes. One of the great walking trail, the North Downs Way, makes this descent, passing right alongside the parish church of Boughton Aluph. A similar network of footpaths and narrow lanes leads southwards to Boughton Lees, which also has a feeling of being stranded in a timeless, smiling landscape.

Westwell
Map 3 ref I6

22 miles W of Dover off the A20

Westwell is a quiet, pretty village located in dense woodland near the larger town of Charing. It was originally a Saxon settlement and developed under the Normans, who built its lovely parish church. On the fringes of the village is a disused watermill which is now a private house but which can be seen clearly from the road. Just outside of Westwell is **Eastwell Park**, with its 40 acre lake providing a counterpoint for the manor house which is now a hotel. On the northern edge of the lake is a ruined church which reputedly houses the bones of Richard Plantagenet, son of Richard III. Local legend has it that he escaped from the Battle of Bosworth field to end his days working anonymously at the Eastwood Estate as a carpenter.

From Dover to Sandwich

Barfreston   *Map 4 ref L5*
10 miles NW of Dover off the A2

A maze of lanes deters heavy traffic from entering Barfreston, a handsome village in the farming country lying just north of the Lyminge Forest. The immediate vicinity was once the site of several collieries, which operated until the Second world War. Nature has taken over again, however, and the dominant feature in the surrounding landscape is farming. Barfreston's small Norman parish church is worth a special visit. It is remarkable for its stone carvings, the best of which are around its east door, representing an array of creatures, scenes of Medieval life and religious symbols. Visitors can obtain an explanatory leaflet from the pub opposite. There is another curious feature of the church - its church bell is attached to a yew tree in the churchyard.

Woolage Green   *Map 4 ref L5*
10 miles NW of Dover off the A2

Rolling hills and wooded countryside lead west from Barfreston and into the hamlet of Woolage Green, where there are interesting footpaths through the fields and woods.

The unspoilt countryside of Woolage Green provides a lovely setting for **The Two Sawyers**, a traditional village pub that is located right on the village green. Open fires provide a warm and bright welcome in the colder months; one of the fireplaces is huge, and dominates one of the bars. Leaded windows add to the palpable sense of tradition, which owners Terry and Jackie Fremantle enhance with old-fashioned conker and pumpkin competitions. The Two Sawyers is a free house, with a large and changing selection of cask ales and

The Two Sawyers

good wines. It also has a good range of bar food, snacks, and fuller meals in the evening. Woolage Green is easily reached, being only 3 km east of the Canterbury to Folkestone Road (the A2). There is ample parking and a choice of B&B accommodation nearby. *The Two Sawyers, Woolage Green, near Canterbury, Kent CT4 6SE Tel: 01304 830295*

Deal
Map 4 ref M5

8 miles N of Dover on the A258

The charming fishing town of Deal has altered very little in character since the 18th century. The fact that its beach is of shingle rather than sand meant that it escaped Victorian development into a full-blown seaside resort of the *"bucket and spade"* variety. The fishing trade has always played a major role along this coastline, and the roots of the industry are still very much in evidence today.

The seafront is one of the most picturesque to be found anywhere on the Southeast coast, and with its quiet alleyways, traditional cottages and houses (many of them colour-washed), and shingle beach festooned with fishing boats, Deal is a delightful place to explore.

The quiet waters just off the coast are known as **The Downs**, and they create a safe natural anchorage for shipping that may otherwise run aground on the treacherous Goodwin Sands. The Sands have been the setting for hundreds of tragic shipwrecks throughout the centuries, and the sad sight of 'drowned' ships with their masts poking above the water is still in evidence at low tide, serving as a permanent reminder of the darker side of the sea.

The sands are mentioned in Shakespeares *"Merchant of Venice"* as a place where the eponymous merchant lost one of his ships. As many as 50,000 men may have perished on these Sands, and there are many tales of *"ghost ships"* having been sighted here.

A good way of learning more about these aspects of the town's past is to take the time to visit its various museums. In St George's Road, in stables once used to house army mules, is the **Maritime and Local History Museum**, where a large collection of models, pictures and other memorabilia relate the maritime history of the town. Also on display are a number of original boats constructed by local boat builders up until the turn of the century. **The Costume and Accessories Museum**, a personal collection of original costumes and accessories put together by Doris Salter, can be found in a private house at 18 Gladstone Road; while in the Town Hall is the **Victoriana Museum**, its displays of toys, dolls, china, ornaments and jewellery from the Victorian and Edwardian eras illustrating the growth of the 19th century souvenir trade.

Deal Castle

You should also look out for the distinctive **Timeball Tower** near the (landward) end of the pier. Built in 1795 to give time signals to ships in the Channel, the four-storey tower had a curious device whereby a black copper ball was dropped down its central shaft to register 1.00pm Greenwich Mean Time each day - so sailors would always know when it was lunchtime! The original timeball was replaced by the modern radio time signal, but a replica ball now drops down the shaft on the hour. On the fourth floor of the building there is a museum devoted to time and telegraphy, including working models.

Close to the Timeball Tower is **Deal Castle** with its distinctive *"lily-pad"* shape (you may have to take an aerial trip to fully appreciate this description!), which was built by Henry VIII during the early 1540's. The castle was actually designed to resemble a Tudor Rose, and was the largest in a chain of five coastal defences built along the south-east coast against possible French invasion. The ruins of another of these, **Sandown Castle**, can be seen at the northern end of town; its few remaining buttresses holding out valiantly against the encroaching sea. Deal Castle was built very specifically as a war bastion, and with 119 guns trained across the sea, it must have been a formidable sight. A permanent exhibition here describes Henry VIII's various castles and their defensive role throughout history.

Walmer   Map 4 ref M5
7 miles N of Dover on the A258

Just to the south of the Castle, Deal merges almost imperceptibly into neighbouring Walmer, and it is interesting to compare the castle here with its larger *"sister"*. **Walmer Castle** was another of Henry VIII's five coastal defences - the other two being Sandgate and Camber (the latter just over the border into East Sussex), which, like Sandown, are both in ruins.

Enjoying a quiet location near Walmer Castle and with fine views over the Channel is **Hardicot Guest House**, which provides a welcoming and restful break for sightseers and cross-channel travellers alike. This detached Victorian house has three guest rooms, two of which command sweeping sea views. There is a similar maritime vista from the garden, which sweeps down towards the sea in a series of tiers. Style and comfort are keynotes at the Hardicot, typified by the chandelier that hangs in the elegant dining room. The proprietors, Mr and Mrs J. W. Stacey, have added a number of imaginative and welcoming touches to the rooms, and guests can sample

Hardicot Guest House

some of their home-made preserves over a leisurely breakfast.
*Hardicot Guest House, Kingsdown Road, Walmer, Kent CT14 8AW
Tel: 01304 373867*

Sandwich   *Map 4 ref M4*
12 miles N of Dover on the A256

Sandwich is one of the ancient Cinque Ports and is a town full of
historical interest. It is not a big place, and one of the best ways of
seeing it is to follow the **Sandwich Town Trail**. Your starting point
is the **Guildhall**, built in 1579 and enlarged in 1912 and in 1973,
when the New Hall and offices were added. It is the third Guildhall,
the previous one being sited on what is now St Peter's churchyard,
and the original having almost certainly stood between King Street
and The Chain, in the area behind the Old Parsonage.

It is well worth taking the time to seek out some of the fascinating historical pieces here in the Guildhall. One of these is the **Moot
Horn**, which is brass and *"of great antiquity"*, and has been used to
summon the people of Sandwich to hear important announcements
from as far back as the 12th century. Today, it is still used to an-
nounce the death of a sovereign and the accession of the new. Then
there is the **Hog Mace**, which, as the name implies, was used to
round up straying animals after the Goose Bell had rung from St

Peter's Church at 4.00am. All such animals, if not repossessed by their owners on payment of a fine, passed to the Brothers and Sisters of St John's Hospital. The evening curfew at 8.00pm is still rung every day, continuing a tradition going back some 800 years.

As you explore the narrow mediaeval streets, you will pass many buildings of historical importance; indeed, the entire town centre has been declared a conservation area. Guarding the northern entrance to the town is the ***Barbican Gate***, a turreted 16th century gatehouse on the quayside. Sandwich is now almost two miles from

The Barbican, Sandwich

the sea, and although its days as a major port have long since passed, it continues to be used as an inland berth by a colourful array of yachts and cruisers. Places that you should make a point of seeing include the Guildhall, the ***Dutch House*** in King Street, ***Strand Street*** with its fine timbered houses, Sandwich's three medieval churches, and ***St Bartholomew's Hospital*** at the far end of New Street, originally founded in the 12th century and consisting of a quadrangle of almshouses grouped around the old chapel.

John Montagu, the 4th Earl of Sandwich, was dissolute and corrupt, but his lasting claim to fame was to order a slice of beef between two pieces of bread as a substitute for a more conventional meal - a snack he could eat without having to leave the gambling table. Thus the Great British Sandwich was born!

CHAPTER SEVEN
Canterbury and the North Coast

Canterbury Cathedral

Chapter 7 - Area Covered

For precise location of places please refer to the colour maps found at the rear of the book.

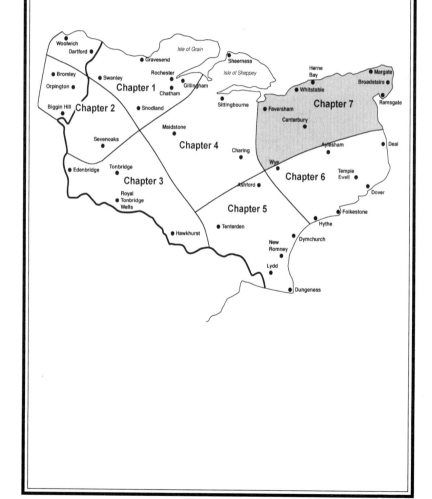

7
Canterbury and the North Coast

Introduction

The northern coast of Kent, extending east from the Isle of Sheppey, is a land of rich historical associations as well as beautiful countryside. Dominated in almost every way by Canterbury and its lovely cathedral, the region has served a historical role as a transit point for human traffic. Some of this traffic was warlike, and the Isle of Thanet, forming the northeastern corner of Kent, was the landfall from which the Saxons began their successful colonisation of the Southeast. Earlier people, some pre-dating the Roman occupation, had already left their mark on the landscape, and archaeologists are constantly finding evidence of prehistoric settlements running all along the coast.

Here, too, Kent's maritime history is brought fully to bear, with the former shipyards of Whitstable and Faversham, now superseded in large part by their yachtsmen descendants, playing a part in the late Middle ages and right through the Tudor period. As in other parts of coastal Kent, particularly those areas facing the Continent, smuggling brought in illicit income and provided a Black Economy long before that economic term found its way into print.

So, from the sacred to the profane, the area around Canterbury has seen more than its share of human activity. Lying somewhere in between are some of its famous residents: Charles Dickens and Sir Edward Heath, John Buchan and Ian Fleming, not forgetting the redoubtable Princess Ermenburga, whose canny deal with her uncle led to the foundation of one of England's first nunneries in the Isle of Thanet. There is a story to be told - or heard - at every turn in this region, and it is not hard to understand how it has cast its spell on travellers for more than two millennia.

Canterbury

Canterbury is one of the loveliest of England's Cathedral cities. Above the walled city soars the *Cathedral*. Its highlights include the central Bell Harry Tower designed by William Westall in the late15th century; Henry Yevele's lofty nave with its magnificent columns; the Trinity Chapel, which houses the splendid tomb of Edward the Black Prince on the south side, and the canopied tomb and alabaster effigies of Henry IV and his queen on the north side; the great north window; and the spectacular Crypt, the largest of any ecclesiastical building in the world.

The Cathedral was founded just after AD 597 by St Augustine after his arrival from Rome. Before his death some seven years later, he had converted large numbers of the native Saxons to Christianity, and Canterbury became the seat of the Mother Church of the Anglicans. Today, the Archbishops of the Cathedral are the Primates of All England, attending all royal functions, and the present incumbent, Dr George Carey, is the 103rd Archbishop of Canterbury.

Canterbury Cathedral

Nothing now remains of the original, pre-conquest buildings; the present Cathedral having been constructed between 1071 and 1500.

This is the Cathedral that witnessed the treacherous murder of Archbishop Thomas Becket on its steps, slain by Henry II's knights. The simple stone marking the spot states that Becket *"died here Tuesday 29th December 1170"*. Although the knights apparently *"misinterpreted"* the King's wishes, the horror has rung down the centuries, and as you walk through the hushed Cathedral this monstrous act is never far from your mind. A penitent Henry, full of remorse for the death of his former friend, came later as a pilgrim to Becket's shrine. Becket's magnificent tomb was destroyed during the Dissolution of the Monasteries in 1538, but visitors to the Cathedral can still see the Altar of the Swordpoint, commemorating the spot where the sword of one of his assassins shattered on the stone floor.

Canterbury is a compact city, and a short walk in any direction will bring you into contact with some part of its history. As for shopping, there are few cities in England that offer greater variety. Specialist shops of every kind stand side by side with all the familiar high street names (many of these can be found in the attractive covered **Marlowe Arcade** in St Margaret's Street), and surprisingly, neither look out of place in their medieval surroundings. However, if you can tear your gaze away from the shop windows every once in a while to look up above street level, you will find just as much to delight the eye there too; for although Canterbury's foremost architectural gems are well marked and easy to spot, many surprises crop up in unexpected places and, like the proverbial two-thirds of the iceberg, will elude the unobservant sightseer altogether. A good example of this is the glorious *"chequer-board"* effect above the entrance to the **Beaney Institute** at the end of the High Street, a splendidly ornate Victorian building which houses the public library, the **Royal Museum** and **Art Gallery**, and the **Buffs Regimental Museum**.

From the bridge you can see the ducking-stool once used to immerse all manner of miscreants - as the sign implicitly warns: *"Unfaithful Wives beware; Butchers Bakers Brewers Apothecaries and all who give short measure"*. The bridge is now a favourite haunt for a motley collection of buskers, who go down well with passing tourists but are not quite so popular with the captive audience of local traders who have become intimately familiar with the repertoire! Opposite The Weavers' you can descend a flight of stone steps below street level to explore the vaults of the 12th century

Eastbridge Hospital, founded in 1180 by Edward Fitzodbold as a hostel for poor pilgrims visiting St Thomas's tomb.

The Poor Priests' Hospital in Stour Street dates back to the 14th century and was used as an almshouse for elderly clergy. It now houses the award-winning ***Canterbury Heritage Museum***, which tells the story of the city from Roman times to the present day, making effective use of the latest computer, hologram and audio-visual technology. Highlights include an exciting video on the story of Thomas Becket, made by local celebrity and master-pupeteer Oliver Postgate, creator of many popular children's television programmes; an audio-visual presentation on Canterbury during the Blitz; and displays and memorabilia concerning Mary Tourtel, the creator of Rupert Bear, who was born at 52 Palace Street in 1874.

Those who like their history to be liberally spiced with fun should also make a point of visiting ***The Canterbury Tales***, which is housed in a medieval church in St Margaret's Street. Here you can enjoy superb recreations of scenes from life in the Middle Ages, all based on Chaucer's famous stories. The minute attention to detail which has been lavished on the models and their clothing and utensils is admirable, and the

The Canterbury Tales

authentic sounds and smells of life in the 14th century abound. There is also a coffee shop and an excellent gift shop, and commentaries in several European languages are available.

Canterbury is also renowned as a centre for the arts, the main event being the annual ***Canterbury Festival*** in autumn, when a varied programme of music, drama, dance, film, exhibitions, walks, talks and community events takes place. Among the many places which play host to these events are the ***Gulbenkian Theatre*** at the University of Kent (reached by heading west from the city centre along St Dunstan's Street and London Road), and Canterbury's major theatrical venue, the ***Marlowe Theatre***, re-located in recent years to The Friars, off St Peter's Street.

This is named after the playwright Christopher Marlowe, who was born in Canterbury in 1564. A contemporary of Shakespeare (who he most probably knew) his works include *"Dr. Faustus"* and *"Tamurlane the Great"*. He attended the **King's School** to the north of Mint Yard in the Cathedral precincts, whose Norman staircase is, incidentally, one of the most famous examples of Norman architecture in England, then went up to Benet (now Corpus Christi) College at Cambridge. As a friend of Sir Francis Walsingham, Elizabeth I's Secretary of State, he supplemented his literary career by taking an active role as a spy. At only 29 years of age, he was stabbed to death in Deptford following what was officially referred to as a tavern brawl, but was more likely to have been a deliberately planned assassination. He is buried at the church of St Nicholas, and church records simply state: *"Christopher Marlowe, slain by ffrancis Archer 1 June 1593"*.

The modest exterior of **The Tasty Spice** belies the spacious interior of this lovely restaurant just opposite St Augustine's Abbey and only five minutes' walk from Canterbury Cathedral. Despite its narrow front the restaurant is able to seat up to 80 people comfortably. Among those who come - and regularly return - to sample the premium-quality Indian cuisine are many celebrities, including the a recent visit from the touring south African cricket team. Mr Rahman, the owner of the Tasty Spice, is a seasoned restaurateur, with more than 20 years' experience. While on the one hand able to satisfy those customers who crave the lesser-known or fiery Indian dishes, on the other he is able to present some imaginative choices for those who are unfamiliar with Indian cuisine. *The Tasty Spice, 9 Longport, Canterbury, Kent CT1 1PE Tel: 01227 463326*

The Tasty Spice

A choice position on the New Dover Road gave **The Old Gate Inn** a prime location as a coaching inn when it was established in 1728. At that time it was known as The Sign of the Gate because of the toll-gate nearby. Hundreds of years of experience welcoming thirsty travellers have helped create the inviting, yet unhurried and relaxed atmosphere of today's inn. Blazing fires greet customers, and old paintings and interesting curios hang from the walls. Landlords Paul and Christine McCrea-Hendicott are experienced publicans with a long association with the pub - Paul's (several times removed)

The Old Gate Inn

cousin James Stevens took control in 1871. Apart from an admirable selection of ales and beers the Old Gate Inn is noted for its food. Up to 165 diners - and another 90 in the garden in back - can avail of the hearty dishes each day from noon. Just as enticing is the chance to have breakfast, or just a cup of coffee, in the morning from 7.30 (8.00 on Sunday). The Old Gate Inn is easy to find from the A2 and there is ample parking in the back. *The Old Gate Inn, 162/164 New Dover Road, Canterbury, Kent CT1 3EL   Tel: 01227 452154, Fax: 01227 456561*

Conveniently located on the south side of Canterbury is **The Phoenix**, a welcoming pub that is within handy walking distance of the city centre, the County Cricket ground, and Canterbury East Railway station. Hanging baskets and a comfortable patio set a cheerful tone outside, while visitors stepping inside are drawn into a cosy world of real ales, comfortable seats, and board games - presided over by two cats who seem to think they own the place. There is home-cooked food lunchtimes and evenings. The pub was originally known as the Bridge House Tavern, but it acquired its present name - quite understandably - when it was rebuilt after a serious fire in

The Phoenix

1961. Managers Neil Bailey and Judy Hodson make every effort to welcome patrons, and their enthusiasm for music and film can come in handy for sly competitors locked in a game of Trivial Pursuit. A timely bought round of drinks might make a difference in the scoring. *The Phoenix, 67 Old Dover Road, Canterbury, Kent CT1 3DB Tel: 01227 464220*

Providing a quiet oasis just ten minutes' walk from the heart of Canterbury is ***Thanington Hotel***, which is an imposing town house - although originally built as a farmhouse - dating from around 1800. Guests have an immediate sense of being welcomed and pampered, and the choice of rooms caters for those who either prefer the ground floor or perhaps have hankered after sleeping in a genuine four-

Thanington Hotel

poster. Jill and David Jenkins preside over a professional staff who are pleased to offer travelling advice or help with reservations locally. Generously proportioned public rooms make a relaxing destination after a day's sightseeing, and guests can also avail of the games room and indoor heated swimming pool. The Thanington Hotel is an ideal base for a walking - or driving - tour of Canterbury and its environs. *Thanington Hotel, 140 Wincheap, Canterbury, Kent CT1 3RY Tel: 01227 453225*

Around Canterbury

Fordwich
Map 4 ref K4

3 miles E of Canterbury on the A28

Fordwich was once a busy port - serving all of Canterbury's trade - on the River Stour, which is tidal up this point. In later years, the river silted up and the deeper draught of commercial shipping vessels robbed Fordwich of its major economic activity. Today the river is still navigable, but only for canoes, which ply their way along the Stour by the town. The partly Norman **Church of St Mary** has a sculptured tomb in which, it is said, St Augustine was once lain. The ancient timbered **Town Hall** retains its Tudor appearance, with its distinctive red roof and half-timbered architecture. It stands beside the quay, where there is still a **ducking stool**, formerly used to duck *"scolds"*.

Littlebourne
Map 4 ref K4

3 miles E of Canterbury off the A257

Littlebourne is an attractive village on the banks of the Little Stour, just to the east of Canterbury. It makes an excellent base from which to explore **Howletts Zoo Park**, set in the grounds of Howletts, an 18th century house with an excellent portico. Having built up a collection of animals from around the world John Aspinall opened the Zoo Park in 1975 with the twin aims of displaying exotic animals in well-maintained surroundings as well as breeding them. Today the parklands are the home of nearly 50 species, including the dhole (an Asiatic wild dog) and the Calamian deer from the Philippines.

Visitors to Littlebourne, near Canterbury are invariably charmed by the **Anchor Inn**, which is permeated with the twin Kent atmospheres of hop-growing and maritime history. There is a story behind the large car park, which sheds light on the pub's interesting history. The Anchor was built in 1623 and originally served as a farm

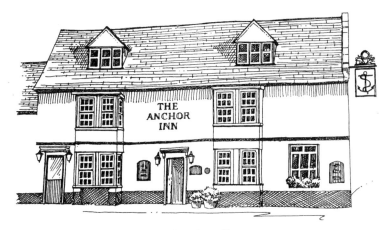

The Anchor Inn

dwelling. In 1694 it became a coaching house, and the large area once given over to stabling horses has now become the car park and large garden. A converted stable now serves as a restaurant on two floors, with original beams upstairs. The extensive menu features local produce and is backed up by a wide-ranging wine list. The pub itself, which is as popular with ramblers as it is with locals, has a good selection of real ales, with a games room as well as traditional bat trap outside in the summer. The walls are adorned with old sepia photographs of the area, interspersed with local hop bines and sailors' knots. *The Anchor Inn, 2 Bekesbourne Lane, Littlebourne, Canterbury, Kent CT3 1UY   Tel: 01227 721207*

Patrixbourne

Map 4 ref K5

4 miles SE of Canterbury off the A2

Patrixbourne is an example of the sort of architectural development espoused by Prince Charles. The village is handsome, with a range of houses dating largely from the 17th to 18th centuries. Recently, however, there was the need for more housing and the planners hit upon the idea of building the new dwellings in the form of a neo-Georgian close. The results are admirable, and blend harmoniously with the existing structures to maintain a sense of unity. Patrixbourne is also noted for its lovely Norman **parish church**, which has some wonderful carvings reminiscent of the church further south in Barfreston. A particularly good example is the priest's door, with a disfigured saint's head above it. There is also some interesting early stained glass including some 16th and 17th century Swiss windows.

Bridge
Map 4 ref K5

5 miles SE of Canterbury off the A2

Bridge stands at a river crossing of the old Dover Road leading from London. Local people found the constant stream of heavy traffic intolerable and mounted a concerted campaign to have the road re-routed past their village. Village solidarity was so strong that in one protest some 1000 people joined the protest to stop traffic for an hour, creating a bottleneck so large that it made national headlines. The government was forced to take action and in 1976 a new bypass opened, offering the sorely needed relief. Near the bridge is a mansion which was altered for Count Zabrowski of *"Chitty Chitty Bang Bang"* fame.

Wingham
Map 4 ref L4

8 miles E of Canterbury on the A257

Wingham is a large village - almost town-sized - with a long tree-lined high street running through its length. On either side of the High Street stand some fine old houses, many of which date back to Tudor times. There is an interesting story surrounding the wooden arcade of the parish church. By the 16th century this Norman church had fallen into a state of acute disrepair. A certain George Ffoggarde, a local brewer, obtained a licence to collect funds for its repair but he embezzled all £244 of it. The intended (costly) stone arcade which was to feature in the repairs had to be carried out in the much cheaper medium of wood.

West to Faversham

Chilham
Map 3 ref J5

6 miles SW of Canterbury on the A252

Chilham is a well-preserved village which just manages to retain a sense of being a working village without seeming too self-conscious about its preserved appearance. The houses are primarily Tudor or Jacobean, with projecting gables and undulating roofs. The village rises to an airy and spacious square, around which houses of different periods blend perfectly. The parish church of St Mary is a good example of Perpendicular Gothic style; its stone and flint tower is particularly attractive.

Chilham Castle is now privately owned and not open to the public, but its spacious grounds can be seen from the road along with elements of the Jacobean mansion. It was near Chilham that the Romans fought their last great battle in Britain. The site is known as Julieberrie Downs in honour of Julius Laberius who was killed in 54BC.

The sign indicating *"XVth Century"* on the whitewashed exterior of **The White Horse** is no idle boast. Records show that this lovely village inn was built in 1422, the final year of the reign of Henry V. The brick frontage, although handsome, gives no real indication of the pub's long history. Inside is a different matter; the Tudor interior features centuries-old beams and an inglenook fireplace that has been dated at 1460. The blazing fires reinforce the sense of cosiness and general warmth. The white Horse is no theme pub, though,

The White Horse

and managers Roy and Joan Terry ensure that it maintains its role as a village amenity for the people of Chilham. There is a good range of pub food and light meals to complement the real ales and wine selection, and the blackboard features daily - and often seasonal - specials. In warmer months customers can relax in the rustic garden or sip a drink at one of the benches and tables facing the square. *The White Horse, The Square, Chilham, near Canterbury, Kent CT4 8BY Tel: 01227 730355.*

Challock   *Map 3 ref I5*
11 miles SW of Canterbury on the A252

The pretty village of Challock is set in the dense woodlands known as **Challock Forest**. Like so many villages with Medieval roots, it was built around its church in a forest clearing. When the Black Plague struck, however, the villagers moved to a new site about a mile from the church. The church, dedicated to Saints Cosmus and Damian, had another brush with bad luck when it was the victim of a direct hit from a German bomb during the Second World War. Now restored, it is worth visiting, particularly to view the inspired wall paintings done in the 1950's as part of the restoration.

Selling   *Map 3 ref I4*
12 miles W of Canterbury off the A2

Selling is a pretty village set in thick woodlands well away from any major roads. It was once, however, something of a transit point for traffic heading from Canterbury to Faversham; the White Lion Inn, a 400 year-old coaching inn, is evidence of this trade. The countryside all around Selling is an attractive mixture of orchard and woodland, particularly heading south towards **Perry Wood**, which has many footpaths criss-crossing its 150 acres of woodland.

The Rose and Crown is a freehouse perched at the top of Crown Hill and bordered by the 150 acres of Perry Wood. This natural woodland is criss-crossed by many footpaths which lead to an Iron Age earthworks and to the famous *"Pulpit"*, with its far-reaching views over the neighbouring villages. The 16th century pub is mellow and inviting, with two inglenook fireplaces, which either crackle in the winter or overflow with floral displays in the summer. Local hops

The Rose and Crown

garland the beams of the bar and there is a unique collection of corn dollies. The flowers inside are only a taste of what is on offer outside, and many rate the cottage-style garden of the Rose and Crown as the best in Kent. It is not wholly given over to flowers, though. There is a traditional bat and trap pitch, a children's play area, and even an aviary. The Rose and Crown prides itself on its real ales, and there are always four ready on hand pumps. There is also a good selection of food both lunchtimes and in the evening. The ample parking even includes hitching posts for horses. *The Rose and Crown, Perry Wood, Selling, Faversham, Kent ME13 9RY Tel: 01227 752214*

Sheldwich   Map 3 ref I4
12 miles W of Canterbury on the A251
Sheldwich stands at a point where the landscape blends gently from scattered woodlands to open meadows and then orchards and farms. Its parish church, dating from the Norman period, stands in the centre of the village and its squat steeple is visible for some miles particularly from the north in the direction of Faversham.

Hernhill   Map 3 ref J4
9 miles W of Canterbury off the A2
A lovely setting in smiling orchard country gives Hernhill a welcoming aspect, and it is just far enough off the A2 to have a sense of seclusion and tranquillity. In addition to the many commercial orchards in the surrounding countryside there is another horticultural attraction, **Mount Ephraim Gardens**, which comprises 8 acres of garden, including a Japanese rock garden, a small lake, a woodland area and a small walk.

Mount Ephraim Gardens

In the village of Hernhill, just under 3 miles from Faversham is **The Three Horseshoes**, a pub that simply oozes history and atmosphere. Just over three centuries old the pub is built in the style that immediately links it with this part of Kent: the exterior is of brick and white weatherboard and traditional Kent peg tiles have been used on the roof. Outside is a sunny garden scattered with picnic tables and the walnut tree - which predates the pub by a century - still gives a good annual supply. The interior reflects Mike and Vera Skipper's aims in maintaining the best aspects of this pub: the decor is old-fashioned brick and timber, old books line the walls, and the floors are bare wood. There is no music to compete with conversation and laughter and the bitter is served straight from the barrel. Patrons appreciate

The Three Horseshoes

the way in which the ales are kept, and the Three Horseshoes attracts customers from a wide radius. Entertainment, not surprisingly, is simple and traditional - draughts, bar billiards, dominoes, cribbage, darts, and chess. The bar meals are served lunch times and evenings and offer imaginative vegitarian choices. *The Three Horseshoes, 46 Staple Street, Hernhill, Faversham, Kent ME13 9UA   Tel: 01227 750842*

Faversham

12 miles W of Canterbury on the A2

Map 3 ref I4

Faversham came as a complete surprise to us, for as you make the long approach from Sittingbourne along the A2 past fields and orchards, there is little to suggest just how charming the heart of Faversham will turn out to be. It still functions as a port today, and boats loaded with timber sail up Faversham Creek, a tributary of the River Swale. It was known as the *"King's port"* during the reign of Edward I, and had been highly favoured by English monarchs for centuries. Great warships were built here, and the medieval warehouses still stand today. At various times in its history, Faversham has traded in everything from oysters to gunpowder, and it has not been adverse to indulging in smuggling activities either. King Stephen established the **Abbey of the Holy Saviour** here, and is said to be buried in an unmarked tomb in the parish church. Sadly, with the Dissolution of the Monasteries, the Abbey virtually disappeared.

The Market Place boasts a splendid **Guildhall**, which sits solidly on an arcade that was built around 1574. Market days still play an important part in the life of the town, and are held on Tuesdays, Fridays and Saturdays beneath the Guildhall. Charming pastel-washed cottages blend in quite comfortably with the elegant Georgian dwellings nearby, and this pleasing mixture of styles adds greatly to the character of the town.

Faversham has over 400 listed buildings; a sure indication that this is a prime historic town. For full details of Faversham's fascinating heritage, the best of its buildings and guided walks available around the town, it is worth making a trip to the **Fleur de Lis Heritage Centre** in Preston Street.

Ospringe   *Map 3 ref I4*
1 mile W of Faversham on the A2

Ospringe straddles the A2 on the outskirts of Faverhsam but can claim a separate pedigree from its larger neighbour. Here, near the north coast of Kent, was a thriving Roman settlement and there have been numerous coins, medallions and household items unearthed to bear witness to its large population. In the centre of the village, on the corner of Water Lane, is a lovely half-timbered medieval building known as the **Maison Dieu**. It served as a combination hospital and hostel for pilgrims on their way to Canterbury. In parts

Maison Dieu, Ospringe

dating from the 13th century it has stout beamed ceilings dating from the Tudor era. Inside lies a museum tracing the history of the area from Roman times, through the Saxon and Medieval period and including some fascinating information about the house itself.

Although only 500 yards from the busy A2 between Sittingbourne and Faversham, ***The Plough Inn*** is a genuine hidden gem. It is a throwback to the days when time was measured by the passing of the sun and the seasons, long before the advent of contraflows, mobile phones, and pagers. The building dates from 1260 and it has been a pub since the mid-18th century. The lovely exterior features include black shutters and trellises offsetting the overall white of

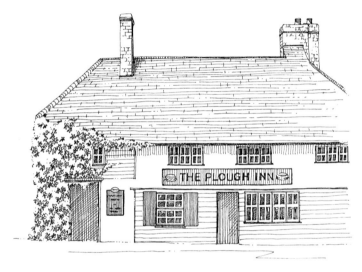

The Plough Inn

the front and the picket fence. The peg-tiled front is as old as the building itself. The garden, with its magnificent hanging baskets, was named the 1997 Shepherd Neame Pub Garden of the Year. Inside there are hop bines hanging from the low oak beams and a wealth of agricultural memorabilia adorning the free space. There is even a 1910 cash register behind the bar. The overall effect is one of timeless warmth, increased by the blazes in the inglenook fireplace. The Plough has an enviable selection of fish specialities among its menu choices, with particularly imaginative preparations of the less commonly served varieties such as mullet and halibut. *The Plough Inn, Lewson Street, Norton, Near Faversham, Kent ME9 9JJ Tel: 01795 521348*

Along the coast to Ramsgate

Whitstable *Map 3 ref J3*
11 miles N of Canterbury on the A290

As you wander round the busy commercial harbour (originally serving as a port of Canterbury) and down its old-fashioned streets lined with fisherman's cottages and linked by a fascinating maze of narrow alleyways, you soon begin to realise that Whitstable is no seaside resort with traditional seaside entertainments, but very much a working town by, and of, the sea. The best way to get the authentic *"flavour"* of Whitstable itself is to take a stroll along the beach behind the Royal Native Oyster Stores and the Pearsons Arms, both of which serve an excellent variety of seafood dishes. From here you can head east towards the harbour or west towards Seasalter, and in both directions you will pass the tightly packed rows of traditional black tarred oyster sheds and weatherboarded cottages that give the town so much of its atmosphere. There are always plenty of activities going on, with fishing boats and barges leaving the harbour, the wet-suit brigade energetically indulging in the host of watersports for which Whitstable is renowned, and hordes of seagulls wheeling and screaming over the piles of discarded oyster shells and crabs.

Over the past few years, a lot of effort has been put into recapturing the charm of bygone Whitstable and preserving its heritage, and full marks must go to the Council and the various local organisations (notably the Whitstable Society and the Whitstable Improvement Trust) who have worked so hard together to make this possible. Residential streets have been closed to traffic at one end to reduce congestion, raised flower beds have been planted in many places, and nice little touches like the wonderful carved benches with maritime themes in **Harbour Street** and on the beach itself all add to the appearance and interest of the town.

Also of note is **Whitstable Castle**, otherwise known as Tankerton Tower, originally built as an octagonal *"folly tower"* by Charles Pearson in 1792 and added to extensively 28 years later by his son. More recently it housed the old district council offices, and it is currently used as a Community Centre.

One of the best places to sample some of the renowned Whitstable fish catch is **Giovanni's**, an award-winning Italian restaurant which draws patrons from the whole Medway area and points far beyond. The restaurant occupies five former houses, giving the interior a

Giovanni's

lovely sense of space - easily enough to seat 80 in real comfort. The distinctive green canopy outside is reprised in the interior decor, with its soothing green wash walls. Fish is given pride of place, and prepared in the finest Italian tradition. Specialities include scallops wrapped in bacon mixed with mushroom, sea bass, baby turbot, and lobster. Those with a taste for more terrestrial fare never leave disappointed, and wild boar - from Devon - is often on the menu. The wine list has been chosen with care and imagination, and here again an Italian flavour shines through, including the excellent house wine. Giovanni Ferrari is a native of Milan and trained at the Palace in St Moritz, Switzerland. He opened this restaurant in 1968 and has gone from strength to strength - just look at the array of international catering awards that adorn the walls. *Giovanni's, 49-55 Canterbury Road, Whitstable, Kent CT5 4HH   Tel: 01227 273034*

Herne Bay
Map 4 ref K3

11 miles N of Canterbury on the A299

Originally a fishing village which developed a notorious reputation for its smuggling activities, Herne Bay is one of the main resorts on the North Kent coast. It was a favourite holiday haven for the Victorian middle classes, and still retains the quiet atmosphere of that particular era - most of the town having been laid out no more than 150 years ago. The town's main landmark is the **Clock Tower** on the promenade; solid, dependable, and just a little preposterous, it stands 80 feet high and was erected in 1836 by a wealthy Londoner, Mrs Anne Thwaytes, to commemorate Queen Victoria's coronation.

Reculver   *Map 4 ref K3*
14 miles NE of Canterbury off the A299

From the promenade of Herne Bay, and from many other parts of the coast and certain stretches of the Thanet Way, your eyes will be drawn again and again to the distinctive silhouette of **Reculver Towers**, standing proud above the rocky beach at Reculver like a pair of giant binoculars.

Reculver is the site of the *Roman Regulbium*, one of the forts built in the 3rd century AD to defend the shore from Saxon invasion. There are only the scantiest remains of this fortress left now, partly because of the incessant erosion and also because the site was taken over as a place of Christian worship, and typically, the earlier structure provided the building materials. The Saxons built a church on the site in the 7th century and five centuries later it was expanded by the Normans. The Normans built the two huge Towers and the west front, which remain almost intact.

It was only through the intervention of Trinity House officials that the church was saved from complete demolition in the 19th century, when the local vicar had begun tearing down the church, which he considered too remote for his parishioners. Trinity House took over the West Front and the Towers, which have continued to serve as landmarks for London-bound shipping. The new church, built out of what Trinity House did not salvage from the old church, can be seen at **Hillborough**, about a mile inland from Reculver.

As a major historic site, Reculver has of course been a happy hunting ground for archaeologists for many years. A grim discovery was made during excavations in the 1960's, when several tiny skeletons were found not far from the Towers. One shudders to dwell on the grisly events which led to their demise some time in Reculver's ancient past, but it is generally believed that these babies were buried alive as human sacrifices. This perhaps lends support to the old legend that local residents are kept awake on stormy nights by the pitiful crying of infants.

Minster-in-Thanet   *Map 4 ref M3*
18 miles E of Canterbury off the A253

Minster-in-Thanet takes its name from the Isle of Thanet, the northeast corner of Kent which was once separated from the mainland by the Wanstum Channel. It is likely that there were settlements here before the Roman era, and it is generally accepted that the Isle of Thanet was the first landfall for invading Saxons.

There are many old buildings in Minster, some of them dating from the Medieval period. The **Old House** was built in 1350 and the **Oak House**, located nearby, is probably almost as old. One of England's first nunneries was established here in the 7th century, on land granted to Princess Ermenburga, who is usually better known by her religious name of Domneva. The land was granted by her uncle, King Egbert, in as *wergild* (compensation) for the murder of her two brothers by his thane Thunor. The princess demanded such land as could be encompassed by her pet hind at a single run. Thunor, alarmed by the amount of land being covered by the hind and attempting to halt it, fell with his horse into a ditch and was drowned - or so legend has it. In the end the hind completed a course that covered more than 1,000 acres. The story is illustrated in the windows of the parish **Church of St Mary**.

The nunnery was later sacked by the Danes and later still came into the hands of the monks of St Augustine's Canterbury. They rebuilt it and added a grange, now called Minster Abbey. Much of the Norman work can still be seen in the cloisters and other parts of the ruins - the Abbey was one of the many victims of Henry VIII's Dissolution.

Situated just west of the Minster and bordered on three sides by the sea, **The Bell Inn** has already enough going for it to make it worth a stop. Add to these considerations its welcoming atmosphere

The Bell Inn

- a loyal local clientele is always a good sign - and the reasons to stop are compelling. Visitors step inside to enter the world of low oak-beam ceilings, blazing log fires, and a murmur of conversation that is occasionally punctuated with a heartfelt laugh. This is a pub that knows how to look after its real ales, and there is a good selection. A good choice of bar snacks, with home-made dishes and daily specials, satisfies lunchtime patrons and the evening a la carte menu offers a selection of dishes at competitive prices. Dining is on two levels, and smoking is off-limits in the upstairs *"barn"* room. The lovely garden is popular in the warmer months, with patrons lingering over their drinks while they drink in the memorable views, or simply bask in the sunshine. *The Bell Inn, 2 High Street, Minster, Kent CT12 4BU   Tel: 01843 821274*

Enjoying a peaceful and secluded setting, ***Wayside Caravan Park*** is only 3 miles from the nearest beach and half a mile from the historic village of Minster. Being small and privately owned are the other attractive features of this prestigious park, and visitors willingly forgo the idea of bars and clubhouses in favour of well-appointed modern caravans. There is a wide range of caravans in the fleet, and the owners are able to cater to the needs of any group - large or small. It's the little things that count here, like the sense of space and tranquillity and the tea tray - or bottle of wine, for

Wayside Caravan Park

longer stays - that greets guests on arriving. There is ample opportunity for sightseeing, eating out, and stocking up on provisions in the attractive towns and villages nearby. and with Ramsgate only 3 miles away, guests can pop over to the continent for a day trip to give a more exotic flavour to their shopping. *Wayside Caravan Park, Way Hill, Minster-in-Thanet, near Ramsgate, Kent CT12 4HW Tel: 01843 821272*

Manston
Map 4 ref M3

19 miles E of Canterbury off the A253

Manston lies just inside the Isle of Thanet, set amid rich farmlands, which are given over to intensive market gardening. The sleepy village came to life with a start in the Second World War, when it became one of the RAF's most prominent airfields in the Battle of Britain.

The Spitfire and Hurricane Memorial Building, housed in RAF Manston, is one of the few surviving operational airfields which figured in the Battle of Britain. Manston was the closest airfield to the enemy coast and consequently bore the brunt of the early Luftwaffe air attacks. The Memorial Building does not charge admission, but its totally self-funding status means that a range of

The Spitfire and Hurricane Memorial Building

aviation-related items are on sale. Some of the most popular are the framed prints of these heroic aircraft, including a number of limited editions. The main attractions, of course, are the two aircraft themselves. TB 752 is one of the few surviving Spitfires with a wartime record, details of which are recorded in a booklet on sale at the sales counter. Its companion, LF 751, is a fine example of Hawker Hurricane. Like the Spitfire it is in excellent condition, thanks in large part to the efforts of the Medway Aircraft Preservation Society (MAPS). Visitors can reflect on the heroic events of 1940 in the Merlin Cafeteria, which has fine views across the airfield, particularly from the patio area. *The Spitfire and Hurricane Memorial Building, Royal Air Force Manston, Ramsgate, Kent CT12 5BS Tel: 01843 823351, extension 2219*

Birchington
Map 4 ref L3
14 miles E of Canterbury on the A28

Birchington is a residential area on the top of low cliffs at the western end of the Margate conurbation. It is primarily a seaside resort, which has become a particular favourite for families with young children. At *All Saints Church*, however, is a monument to one of the most famous British artists of the 19th century. Here, at the doorway, is buried Dante Gabriel Rossetti, the poet and artist who was instrumental in the formation of the Pre-Raphaelite Brotherhood. A memorial stone, carved by his mentor Ford Madox Brown, marks the grave.

At *Quex Park*, about a half-mile south of the village, is mansion containing the nine-gallery Powell-Cotton museum of natural history and the distinctive Waterloo Bell Tower built in 1819.

Margate
Map 4 ref M2
16 miles E of Canterbury on the A28

Margate is a town that fulfils most people's expectations of the typical English seaside resort. Long sweeping stretches of golden sand, promenades, amusement arcades, candyfloss and fun fairs. In bygone days, the resort was a Mecca for the day-tripper from London (greatly assisted by excellent water-transport along the River Thames), and there are still those faithful patrons who come back year after year. The covered bathing machine was invented in Margate in 1753 by a Quaker and glovemaker called Benjamin Beale.

Tudor House, in King Street, was built in the early 16th century during the reign of Henry VIII, and now contains an exhibition on the human occupation of Thanet from earliest times through to the end of the Tudor period. Half a mile inland on Nash Road is the medieval *Salmestone Grange*, originally a grange or farm of St Augustine's Abbey at Canterbury, and arguably the best-preserved example of a monastic grange in England. The chapel, crypt and kitchen are all open to the public. Along St Peter's Footpath, off College Road, you can also visit *Drapers Windmill* on Sunday afternoons from late-May to mid-September and on Thursday evenings in July and August. This is a black smock windmill built sometime around 1840, now restored to full working order by the Drapers Windmill Trust.

Margate also has two truly *"hidden"* treasures, to be found within a few hundred yards of each other at the eastern end of town. Firstly, there are the *Margate Caves* with their entrance in Northdown Road; enormous caverns which were cut from the chalk cliffs over

1,000 years ago. Used variously as a refuge, a mediaeval dungeon and church, and a hiding place for smugglers and their contraband, the Caves are open daily throughout the summer.

Nearby, off Northdown Road on Grotto Hill, is the **Shell Grotto**. Do not be misled by the name, which may perhaps conjure up visions of a rather twee collection of shell-studded jewellery boxes, housed in somebody's cellar. In fact, the grotto is thought to have pagan origins, and the underground passages and chambers have been skilfully decorated with literally millions of seashells.

Without doubt one of the highest-rated qualifiers among the hidden gems of Kent is **Batchelors**, a lovely patisserie that tempts passers-by along the main road through Cliftonville, near Margate. Franz and Janet Ottiger have run this small business for more than a quarter of a century, tempting the sweet tooth of anyone who passes

Batchelors

near their modest shop front - and providing a reason to return again and again. Franz is the patisserie chef, responsible for a wide range of pastries, cakes, continental breads, and speciality items such as birthday cakes. Snacks are served all day, and Batchelors is a popular spot for a refreshing morning coffee or afternoon tea. With the wonderful aroma of the bakery wafting through into the tea room, though, it is hard to imagine stopping just for a drink. *Batchelors, 246 Northdown Road, Cliftonville, Margate, Kent CT9 2PX   Tel: 01843 221227*

Located near the tip of the Isle of Thanet, and priding itself on being the most easterly farm in Kent, is *East Northdown Farm and Gardens*. This lovely farm, tucked between the North Foreland, St Peters, and Northdown, has been the home of the Friend family for over 500 years.

East Northdown Farm and Gardens

The mild maritime climate ensures that temperatures are moderate, and it is rare for the mercury to dip below -6 in a typical winter. This climatic advantage means that the Isle of Thanet can produce "primeur" (early or winter vegetables) - and it is the nearest such agricultural area to London. East Northdown Farm was the home of the Thanet cauliflower industry in the last century.

The gardens are laid out to capitalise on the other factors that come into play - low annual rainfall, chalky soils, and a drying north-easterly wind. Together these conditions lend themselves to the cultivation of a range of plants from the Mediterranean, Southern Africa, California, and the Far East. The Farmhouse Garden is also the home of the *"Northdown Clawnut"*, the best walnut variety in Britain - grown from a nut by planted by Anne Friend around 1820.

East Northdown Farm and Gardens stocks a comprehensive range of plants suited to coastal and chalky areas as well as local produce. William and Louise Friend are knowledgeable plantsmen and can offer all sorts of advice to struggling gardeners. Children also enjoy a visit to East Northdown Farm - with the play area, pets corner, farmyard animals, and plenty of space. Visitors can sample the refreshments at the Garden Tearooms by the farmhouse, which are open on Saturday afternoons in the early spring and daily in summer. *East Northdown Farm and Gardens, Margate, Kent CT9 3TS Tel: 01843 862060 Fax: 01843 860206*

Broadstairs
Map 4 ref N3

20 miles E of Canterbury on the A255

Broadstairs is probably best known for its associations with Charles Dickens, and visitors who have come in search of Bleak House will find it high up on the cliffs at the northern end of town, overlooking the popular family beach at Viking Bay. The sands of the little harbour here (described by Dickens as *"rare good sands"*) are partly protected by a small 16th century pier, a replacement for one built during the reign of Henry VIII.

Other famous people associated with the town include Sir Edward Heath, who was born here in 1916, and another famous sailor, Sir Alec Rose, who lived here for many years. Frank Richards, the creator of *"Billy Bunter"*, also lived in the town, as did John Buchan, whose popular spy thriller, The Thirty-Nine Steps, would become an even more popular film. He wrote the story at a house called St Cuby on Cliff Promenade, and the staircase that gave him his inspiration still stands opposite the house, its 78 steps halved by Buchan to make a better title. Another native of Broadstairs was the eminent Victorian railway engineer, Thomas Russell Crampton.

Opposite the railway station you will find the **Crampton Tower**, a railway museum dedicated to his life and work, with exhibits of his blueprints, drawings and photographs. The Broadstairs Stagecoach is also on display, and there is a superb 00 guage model railway for all you enthusiasts to enjoy.

Ramsgate
Map 4 ref M3

18 miles E of Canterbury on the A253

The ancient origins of Ramsgate were as a small fishing village, and this it continued to be until the harbour was built in 1749. In 1822 George IV landed here (the **obelisk** on the East Pier commemorates this historic event), and since that time it has adopted the title of *"Royal Harbour"*. By the end of the 19th century, its fishing fleet had grown to become the largest of any port on the south coast of England, and even though the fishing industry fell into decline at the beginning of the First World War and the future of the harbour began to look uncertain, it was soon to enjoy a brief moment of glory that would earn it a permanent place in the history books. This was in 1940, when over 40,000 British troops evacuated from Dunkirk were landed here, snatched from the jaws of death by the brave armada of *"Little Ships"*. The parish church of St George commemorates this important episode in Ramsgate's and England's history with a special stained glass window.

West of the harbour, in the old West Cliff Hall above the Sally Line ferry terminal, is the ***Motor Museum***, where a fascinating range of veteran and vintage cars and motorcycles from Edwardian times to the 1950's are on display. Many famous marques are represented, and there are well over 100 exhibits to enjoy.

Tourist Information Centres

Kent is part of the South East England Tourist Information Centre Network. Each centre, or TIC, provides a wide range of services, including accommodation booking, local events information, travel information and an extensive selection of maps, guides, and brochures.

*Centres in **bold** are open all the year around.*

Ashford
18 The Churchyard, Ashford, Kent TN23 1QG
Tel: 01233 629165 Fax: 01233 639166

Broadstairs
6B High Street, Broadstairs, Kent CT10 1LH
Tel: 01843 862242 Fax: 01843 865650

Canterbury
34 St Margaret's Street, Canterbury, Kent CT1 2TG
Tel: 01227 766567 Fax: 01227 459840

Clacket Lane
Motorway Services (Westbound) M25, Junction 5-6, Westerham Kent TN16 2ER Tel: 01959 565615 Fax: 01959 565617

Cranbrook
Vestry Hall, Stone Street, Cranbrook, Kent TN17 3HA
Tel: 01580 712538

Dartford

The Clocktower, Suffolk Road, Dartford, Kent DA1 1EJ
Tel: 01322 343243

Deal

Town Hall, High Street, Deal, Kent CT14 6BB
Tel: 01304 369576 Fax: 01304 380641

Dover

Townwall Street, Dover, Kent CT16 1JR
Tel: 01304 205108 Fax: 01304 225498

Edenbridge

Stangrove Park, Edenbridge, Kent TN8 5LU
Tel: 01732 868110 Fax: 01732 868114

Faversham

Fleur de Lis Heritage Centre, 13 Preston Street, Faversham
Kent ME13 8NS Tel: 01795 534542

Folkestone

Harbour Street, Folkestone, Kent CT20 1QN
Tel: 01303 258594 Fax: 01303 259754

Gravesend

10 Parrock Street, Gravesend, Kent DA12 1ET
Tel: 01474 337600 Fax: 01474 337601

Herne Bay

12 William Street, Herne Bay, Kent CT6 5EJ
Tel: 01227 361911

Hythe

En Route Building, Red Lion Square, Hythe, Kent CT21 5AU
Tel: 01303 267799 Fax: 01303 260085

Maidstone

The Gatehouse, Palace Gardens, Mill Street , Maidstone
Kent ME16 6YE Tel: 01622 602169 Fax: 01622 673581

Margate

22 High Street, Margate, Kent CT9 1DS
Tel: 01843 220241 Fax: 01843 230099

New Romney

Town Hall House, 35 High Street, New Romney, Kent TN28 8BT
Tel: 01797 364044 Fax: 01797 364194

Ramsgate

19-21 Harbour Street, Ramsgate, Kent CT11 8HA
Tel: 01843 583333 Fax: 01843 591086

Rochester

95 High Street, Rochester, Kent ME1 1LX
Tel: 01634 843666 Fax: 01634 847891

Royal Tunbridge Wells

The Old Fish Market, The Pantiles, Royal Tunbridge Wells
Kent TN2 5TN Tel: 01892 515675 Fax: 01892 534660

Sevenoaks

Buckhurst Lane, Sevenoaks, Kent TN13 1LQ
Tel: 01732 450305 Fax: 01732 461959

Tenterden

Town Hall, High Street, Tenterden, Kent TN30 6AN
Tel: 01580 763572 Fax: 01580 766863

Tonbridge

Castle Street, Tonbridge, Kent TN9 1BG
Tel: 01732 770929 Fax: 01732 770449

Whitstable

7 Oxford Street, Whitstable, Kent CT5 1DB
Tel/Fax: 01227 275482

Index

The Hidden Places Series

ORDER FORM

To order more copies of this title or any of the others in this series
please complete the order form below and send to:

**Travel Publishing Ltd,7a Apollo House, Calleva Park
Aldermaston, Berkshire, RG7 8TN**

	Price	Quantity	Value
Regional Titles			
Channel Islands	£6.99	....	....
Cheshire	£7.99	....	....
Cornwall	£7.99	....	....
Devon	£7.99	....	....
Dorset, Hants & Isle of Wight	£4.95	....	....
East Anglia	£4.95	....	....
Gloucestershire	£6.99	....	....
Heart of England	£4.95	....	....
Kent	£7.99	....	....
Lancashire	£7.99	....	....
Lake District & Cumbria	£7.99	....	....
Northeast Yorkshire	£6.99	....	....
Northumberland & Durham	£6.99	....	....
Nottinghamshire	£6.99	....	....
Peak District	£6.99	....	....
Potteries	£6.99	....	....
Somerset	£6.99	....	....
South East	£4.95	....	....
South Wales	£4.95	....	....
Surrey	£6.99	....	....
Sussex	£6.99	....	....
Thames & Chilterns	£5.99	....	....
Welsh Borders	£5.99	....	....
Wiltshire	£6.99	....	....
Yorkshire Dales	£6.99	....	....
Set of any 5 Regional titles	**£25.00**	....	....
National Titles			
England	£9.99	....	....
Ireland	£8.99	....	....
Scotland	£8.99	....	....
Wales	£8.99	....	....
Set of all 4 National titles	**£28.00**	....	....
	TOTAL	_____	_____

**For orders of less than 4 copies please add £1 per book for
postage & packing. Orders over 4 copies P & P free.**

*PLEASE TURN OVER TO COMPLETE
PAYMENT DETAILS*

The Hidden Places Series
ORDER FORM

Please complete following details:

I wish to pay for this order by:

Cheque: ☐   Switch: ☐

Access: ☐   Visa: ☐

Either:

Card No: ☐☐☐☐ ☐☐☐☐ ☐☐☐☐ ☐☐☐☐

Expiry Date: ☐☐☐

Signature: ....

Or:

I enclose a cheque for £ .... made payable to Travel Publishing Ltd

NAME: ....

ADDRESS: ....

....

....

....

POSTCODE: ....

TEL NO: ....

Please send to:
Travel Publishing Ltd
7a Apollo House
Calleva Park
Aldermaston
Berkshire, RG7 8TN

The Hidden Places Series
READER REACTION FORM

The Hidden Places research team would like to receive reader's comments on any visitor attractions or places reviewed in the book and also recommendations for suitable entries to be included in the next edition. This will help ensure that the **Hidden Places** series continues to provide its readers with useful information on the more interesting, unusual or unique features of each attraction or place ensuring that their stay in the local area is an enjoyable and stimulating experience.

To provide your comments or recommendations would you please complete the forms below as indicated and send to: **The Research Department, Travel Publishing Ltd., 7a Apollo House, Calleva Park, Aldermaston, Reading, RG7 8TN.**

Please tick as appropriate: Comments ☐   Recommendation ☐

Name of *"Hidden Place"*:

Address:

Telephone Number:

Name of Contact:

Comments/Reason for recommendation:

Name of Reader:

Address:

Telephone Number:

The Hidden Places of Kent

The Hidden Places Series
READER REACTION FORM

The Hidden Places research team would like to receive reader's comments on any visitor attractions or places reviewed in the book and also recommendations for suitable entries to be included in the next edition. This will help ensure that the ***Hidden Places*** series continues to provide its readers with useful information on the more interesting, unusual or unique features of each attraction or place ensuring that their stay in the local area is an enjoyable and stimulating experience.

To provide your comments or recommendations would you please complete the forms below as indicated and send to: **The Research Department, Travel Publishing Ltd., 7a Apollo House, Calleva Park, Aldermaston, Reading, RG7 8TN.**

Please tick as appropriate: Comments ☐   Recommendation ☐

Name of *"Hidden Place"*:

Address:

Telephone Number:

Name of Contact:

Comments/Reason for recommendation:

Name of Reader:

Address:

Telephone Number:

Map Section

The following pages of maps encompass the main cities, towns and geographical features of Kent, as well as all the many interesting places featured in the guide. Distances are indicated by the use of scale bars located below each of the maps

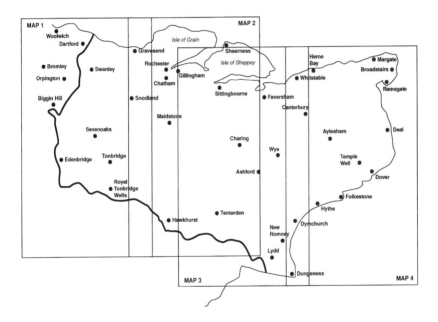

These maps are small scale extracts from the *South East England Tourist Map,* reproduced with kind permission of *Estates Publications.*

MAP 1

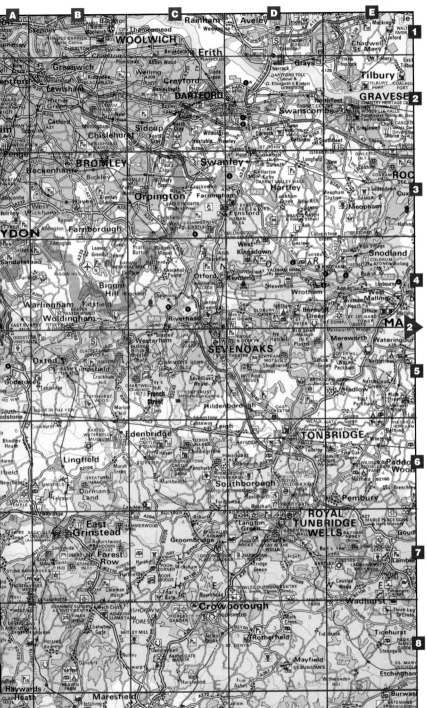

MAP 2

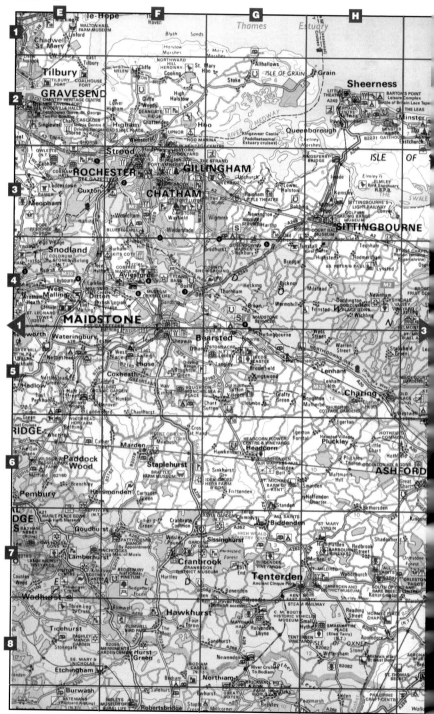

MAP 3

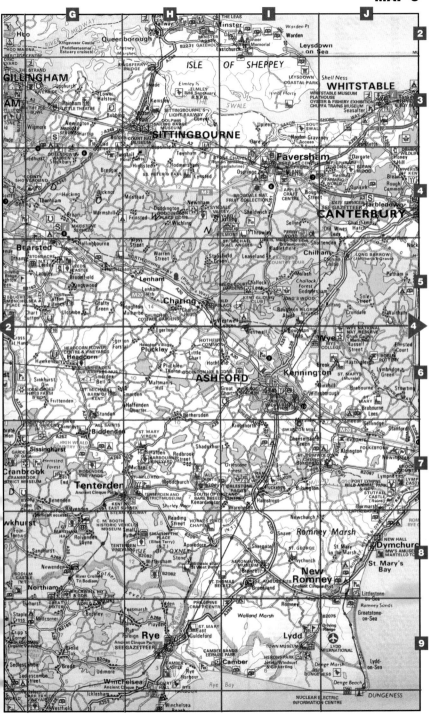

0   1   2   3   4   5 miles
0 1 2 3 4 5 6 7 8 kilometres

MAP 4